D1139276

PINK FLOYD

A Kaleidoscope of Conundrums

Danann
BOOKS

Danann
BOOKS

First Published Danann Publishing Ltd 2017

WARNING: For private domestic use only, any unauthorised Copying, hiring, lending or public performance of this book is illegal.

CAT NO: DAN0346

Written by Michael O'Neill

Copy Editing Tom O'Neill

Photography courtesy of

Getty images

Andrew Whittuck	Waring Abbott
Adam Ritchie	Peter Still/Redferns
Michael Ochs Archives/Stringer	Will/ullstein bild
Gems	Images Press
INA	Ebet Roberts/Redferns
Shinko Music	Rob Verhorst/Redferns
David Redfern	Chip Hires/Gamma-Rapho
Michael Putland	Tony Bock/Toronto Star
Mick Gold/Redferns	Hiroyuki Ito
Nik Wheeler	John D Mchugh/AFP
Ian Dickson/Redferns	Simone Cecchetti/Corbis

Other images - Wikimedia Commons

Book layout & design Darren Grice at Ctrl-d

ISBN: 978-1-912332-02-1

CONTENTS

ONCE UPON A TIME IN CAMBRIDGE

1960s Britain was in the grip of a wave of youth rebellion that saw the old class-stiff, empire-rich stolidness break open to reveal a sumptuous seam of cultural wealth buried beneath the weight of rigidity, convention and privilege. From the ignored realms of working class Britain, brave new voices had risen up through music, art, photography and theatre to challenge the status quo. Amongst this bubbling and foaming of cultural insubordination, fed by a ready availability of mind-altering drugs, it was music, liberated from its staid past and hurled into a bright, feisty future by musicians and singers, that spoke most urgently to the new generation of liberation-hungry youth. The music groups capped themselves with weird names like The Beatles, The Stones, Deep Purple, Procol Harum or the Kinks, putting the fear of anarchy into parents and the voice of authority.

In the UK at the time, London was the undoubted king of the open road to freedom, generously granting favours to its subjects with King's Road, Notting Hill and Carnaby Street, where its maids of honour Twiggy, Mary Quant or Jean Shrimpton might be glimpsed.

But whilst the swinging might have been well under way by the mid-60s, a quiet addition to the upheaval was forming an hour north of the capital. A revolution within a revolution was forming and amongst all of the working-class foment, a gaggle of middle-class boys in the medieval university town of Cambridge, a one hour drive to the north of London, was about to lead popular music away from the rut it had already settled into and along unknown paths, taking a grateful listening public along with it cheering blissfully.

Cambridge was the alma mater of one lad in particular, who was to play Pied Piper to his adoring fans.

He saw the light of day on the 6th of January 1946 at his parents' home close to the town centre. His name was Roger Keith "Syd" Barrett, the fourth of five children born to Max and Winifred. It was Max's interest in music, passed on to his son, that led indirectly to a parting of the ways in 60s popular music.

Cambridge also played nursemaid to two other boys; one of them had moved to the town with his mother after the death of his father in WWII at the Battle of Anzio. His name was George Roger Waters, who had been born in Surrey on the 6th of September 1943. The other boy whose name would be engraved into music history was David Jon Gilmour, who was born in a village just outside of the town on the 6th of March 1946.

The other two men who were to cement the musical phenomenon that was Pink Floyd were Nicholas Berkeley "Nick" Mason, who had been born in Birmingham on the 27th of January 1944, and Richard William "Rick" Wright, born in Middlesex on the 28th of July 1943.

Barrett, Gilmour and Waters met long before pink Floyd Rose to glory. They were enrolled in the Homerton College Art Club for Saturday morning sessions. Barrett was smart, and his energies during his school years were directed towards art, drama and poetry. He was also fearless in defending his opinions, very good-looking and very popular. Many people have attempted to find a correlation between the death of Syd's father in 1961 and his own erratic behaviour later. But having enjoyed a close friendship with Barrett at the time, David Gilmour remembered that Barrett never spoke about his father's death and that he couldn't discern any great alteration in Syd's behaviour afterwards.

Starting his musical career on the ukulele, Syd soon turned to rock 'n' roll and the Höfner acoustic guitar.

Roger was a very talented sportsman, playing both cricket and rugby, but developed a huge antipathy towards the rest of his school life. Most of the teachers he found to be intolerable, teaching in an education system unfit for a new generation and a new era of burgeoning freedom. Waters battled against it. His guitar came from an uncle, but the teenager veered towards jazz and blues and initially avoided rock 'n' roll. His musical preferences, however, were unappreciated at home.

In his late teens, infused with the new air of freedom coming from America, Roger and various friends took off for trips around Europe and the Middle East, experiences that would feed into his music later. In the early 60s, Waters' left-wing politics saw him become chairman in the local youth section of the CND, where he no doubt turned up to meetings in his leather jacket and astride his motorcycle.

Meanwhile, David Gilmour was also enjoying the fruits of an authoritarian grammar school education including attending lessons on Saturday mornings. A clever lad, by his own admission he was a lazy pupil, and it was only the advent of the Everly Brothers that propelled him into action and towards the guitar, borrowed from his next door neighbour. With help from a guitar book by Pete Seeger, a guitar legend took his first tentative steps toward stardom. When Gilmour's father was lured by a professorship to the United States, the young David stayed in Cambridge with another family. Needless to say, musical gigs took priority over his O-level exam studies.

By the time the apparently shy and unassuming Gilmour came to take his A-levels, his parents had moved to the United States permanently, and Gilmour was part of the band he'd helped form known as Jokers Wild. Like Barrett, Gilmour, although more smartly dressed than Syd despite his *"blue jeans with patches on them"*, was a favourite with the girls, and his reputation as a guitarist was also rising rapidly. He even came to the attention of Brian Epstein, who sent a talent scout to watch him.

And what was Richard Wright up to at this time? By the age of twelve, Wright was playing the piano, guitar and trumpet having taught himself the rudiments. Later, he studied the theory and composition of music and became interested in traditional jazz. He often went to gigs to listen to it and was led to considering a musical career by the likes of Miles Davis and Eddie Coltrane. Uncertain of what path to take in life after school, and by his own admission frightened of everything around him, a fact which led him to become quite aggressive, Richard allowed himself to be directed towards an architectural course at the Regent Street Polytechnic in 1962, where he met Nick Mason and Roger Waters.

Nick Mason's family left Birmingham and moved to Hampstead in London finishing his secondary education at the Frensham Heights School in Surrey. By all accounts, he enjoyed his time there even though his attention was also focused more on jazz than on schoolwork. Although lacking

6

any formal training, a fact he regretted, the 14-year-old was serious about his drumming. Later, he, too, would meet his future bandmates Roger Waters, Rick Wright, and Bob Klose, at Regent Street Polytechnic, where he went to study on a five-year course in architecture. He continued drumming, though not driven to become a musician, more interested in cars than anything else.

"Anyone want to start a group?" This was the notice pinned on the college noticeboard by Keith Noble and Clive Metcalfe that brought together Mason and Waters, whose guitar playing was still rather underdeveloped.

There was one other Cambridge boy who would play a role in the establishment of Pink Floyd even though he was never officially a member of the band. This was Rado Robert Garcia Klose, also a jazz and blues enthusiast, whose father had been a refugee from Nazi Germany. Klose came into contact with Waters and Barrett at school in Cambridge before leaving to study architecture in London, but he had known David Gilmour from a very early age.

Inevitably, in an era when the Beatles were filling the airwaves, the boys began to contemplate forming their own bands, and by 1962, Syd was in a band known as Mott and the Mottoes, rehearsing songs by Chuck Berry, Buddy Holly or The Shadows at his house. That was the year that he enrolled at the Cambridge School of Art, where he stayed for two years, enjoying himself enormously, irreverently and loudly and, of course, playing the guitar. More importantly, this was where Syd came into contact with David Gilmour, who was studying modern languages in the adjacent Cambridge College of Art and Technology building. Fellow students remember that Gilmour's guitar seemed to be stuck to his hands; he was never without it.

Whilst Gilmour perfected his solid musicianship, Syd was prone to experimenting — when he wasn't artificially creating disturbances in the classroom, unable to process being told what to do in a normal way, and subject to somewhat irrational rebellions. His mother, too, was a victim of his bullying, which she indulgently allowed to go unchallenged.

At this stage, dope had entered his life; its impossible to say whether this was partly responsible for his *"slightly eccentric"* behaviour. What carried Syd through, however, was what his friends described as his *"charismatic quality"*, a quality that made him very attractive to women in particular; he was different from the other boys of his age. No one knew what happened to him when he would suddenly disappear from parties or groups of friends, reappearing later just as suddenly; and after he had bought his first car, he would drive out to spend time amongst the natural beauty of the surrounding countryside; an unusual pastime in this new, youth-threatened era.

Another unusual pastime was his experimentation with light shows, and in 1963, when Syd Barrett was accepted at the Camberwell School of Art in London, he came into contact with Reg Gadney, who made huge light boxes, thus extending Barrett's path into psychedelia.

Despite the attractions of London life, Syd often returned to Cambridge, picking up the guitar to play with a group known as The Hollerin' Blues, which, by 1965, had morphed into Those Without, still with Syd on guitar.

With that college notice board message from Noble and Metcalfe, Sigma 6 was born, the Russian doll from which Pink Floyd would emerge. Before long, the *"incredibly quiet"* Richard Wright, wearing his black leather jacket and serving up acerbic remarks, had joined them on keyboards, and before the year was out the band had a manager, Ken Chapman. According to Nick Mason, the band was certainly nothing to shout about, but fortunately they continued playing, draping themselves several times over the following year with ever more unappealing names; The Megadeaths or The Screaming Abdabs.

The name was not the only thing that changed; when Bob Klose arrived in London and was absorbed into the

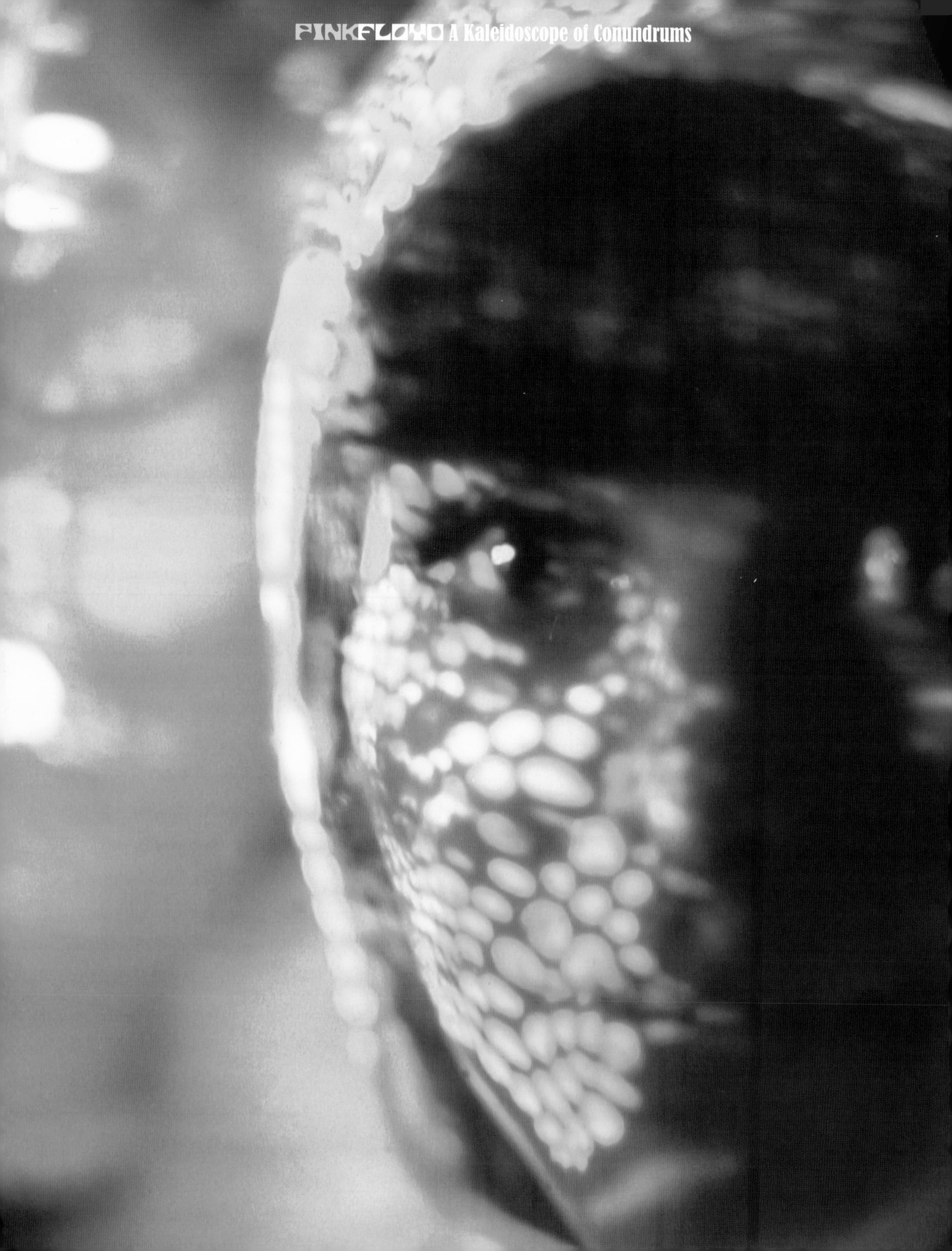

band, his playing style caused Metcalfe and Noble to leave the group and continue as a duo, a change that saw Waters pick up the bass. At the same time, Wright had become so bored at the Polytechnic that he dropped out, and after a period abroad returned home to a course at the Royal College of Music in London.

Waters and Mason, too, were finding student life frustrating, but their musical interests were encouraged by the architecture tutor Mike Leonard, who was not only a pianist but also interested in lighting effects. The two young men had soon moved into Leonard's house as tenants. Into this house, Syd also found his way, sharing a bedroom with Roger Waters. Thus the pieces of the puzzle slowly began to fit together.

The Spectrum Five, as the boys now called themselves, complete with Richard Wright back at the keyboards, were welcome to rehearse on the lower floor of the tutor's house, producing, as Leonard remembers, a *"phenomenal"* noise. One of the problems was the lack of a proper lead singer — before a solution was found in the shape of Chris Dennis, an RAF technician, who fronted the band for the next six months.

9

More band names came and went, inspired by Pink Anderson and Floyd Council, two bluesmen from North Carolina; The Pink Floyd Blues Band and The Pink Floyd Sound. Legend has it that it was Syd who sealed the deal, by simply announcing one day that the band should be called Pink Floyd.

Not long after, Dennis was posted to Bahrain and Barrett took his place in front of the microphone.

NO ONE HEARD THE SOUND OF MUSICAL TECTONIC PLATES SHIFTING AND FAME BECKONING COYLY.

MAIN IMAGE: A young woman in the audience is projected with Pink Floyd's psychedelic light show at the UFO Club, London, December 1966

OUT OF CHAOS
INTO THE LIGHT

As spring turned into summer in 1965, it was time for Bob Klose to pack up his guitar and return to his studies. It was a major shock for the group; Klose was a far better musician than any of the others, but once he had taken his knowledge of the blues with him, the band needed something to fill in the void he had left behind. They had the talent; Syd had started writing songs and experimenting with sounds, inspired by the likes of Pete Townshend; Roger Waters was exploring conceptual work.

Syd, who still returned to Cambridge on occasion, had by now come into contact with LSD and other drugs, a fact becoming more obvious to everyone when he got back to London each time. His new girlfriend, Lindsey Corner, viewed her boyfriend's activities with great leniency, which was not good news for a mercurial spirit like Syd.

Musically, the Pink Floyd Sound, as the lads still billed themselves, were floating in a no man's land of their own, but one which slotted into the avant-garde ambience of the mid-60s. They were still turning out blues songs, but these songs floated in a sea of cosmic vibrancy. When they brought this unusual sound to the Marquee, in 1966, Peter Jenner, then a lecturer at the London School of Economics, heard their exotic sound with growing enthusiasm. Hearing that the band was without management, Jenner knew what his next move was going to be. But the summer holidays, and the prospect of smoking dope on Greek islands proved to be a greater draw than Jenner, and the

band went their separate ways seeking summer relaxation — and in Roger's case, his first acid trip; lasting forty-eight hours on the Greek island of Patmos. It was not acid that began to cause fissures in Roger's relationship with the gentle Richard Wright during that summer, however, but his own insecure demons.

Jenner's patience was rewarded in the autumn with the band's acceptance of his proposal; he negotiated a twelve-month leave of absence from the LSE and together with his friend Andrew King, took over management of Floyd.

Jenner had little knowledge of the music industry, but fortunately his friend King had some inherited money available. So together with their new management team, Syd Barrett, Nick Mason, Roger Waters and Richard Wright shortly found themselves partners in Blackhill Enterprises. Whereupon Barrett, Waters, Mason and Wright finally ditched their studies; a move that caused Barrett to engage in contorted mental arguments for and against doing so. It was the start of long careers in the music business for all of those involved — except, of course, for one man, whose career would be all too short.

Jenny Fabian, author of the 1969 novel Groupie, watched Floyd Play a gig at the All Saints Hall in West London, where not only their treatment of the blues, and Syd's *"magnetic"* performances, but also back projections and coloured slides set the band apart from its competitors. Their songs were reported to be more like improvised psychedelic excursions

12

ABOVE LEFT-RIGHT: Syd Barrett, Rick Wright

14

16

NEXT PAGE: Pink Floyd L-R Nick Mason, Rick Wright,

NEXT PAGE: Pink Floyd L-R Nick Mason, Rick Wright,
Roger Waters and Syd Barrett in 1967 in London

18

preceded by a short introductory theme from a classic tune, because, as Waters once said, we couldn't work out how to play covers… we couldn't play at all, so we had to do something stupid and 'experimental'. It didn't take long for word to spread that there was an exotic new kid on the block and attendances at the hall shot up into the hundreds.

As the band moved forward, Barrett and Waters, who had been songwriting since their Cambridge days, wrote songs for the group, although it was Barrett who turned out the best lyrics; perhaps because he was in a happy, if short-lived, bubble of contentment, surrounded by clouds of dope and girlfriend Lindsay, concentrating on I-Ching, songwriting and playing the guitar.

Their managers set about getting the band into the public eye, and the first thing they needed was a demo for the record companies. So it was into the studio and out with a song by Barrett, inspired by Jenner's humming 'Interstellar Overdrive', and also 'Candy and a Currant Bun', amongst others. Interstellar Overdrive found its way onto the soundtrack of the film 'San Francisco' by Anthony Stern. A first Floyd strike at the mainstream.

In December 1966, another brick in the path to success was set down when the UFO Club opened its doors in London with showers of primitive coloured lighting effects playing across the musicians of Pink Floyd and The Soft Machine. The two groups became the in-house bands and established their reputations at the same time, as they played to youngsters floating about high on acid or zoned out on the floorboards. According to most people, the main element keeping Floyd afloat musically was enigmatic Syd, pouring out his indefinable guitar riffs as the shadows curled over him, supported by Wright's ethereal keyboard trying to compete with the bass of Roger Waters. It was the reserved Richard Wright who was the unsung hero of the group, though; underestimated by everyone, it was he who made the harmonies work; it was he who made the voices gel. And it was his keyboard work that wrapped the songs in coloured psychedelia.

As their reputation fanned out, Jenner was almost able to

20

celebrate a deal with Polydor Records. Just before signing a contract, however, he decided instead to engage with whizz-kid booking agent Bryan Morrison, who talked him out of the Polydor deal. Morrison had connections, and the most important of them was to the record label EMI. So it was that Pink Floyd found themselves with an album contract and a £5000 advance, as the hip kids in the venerable organisation. They were on their way.

On the 11th of March 1967, Pink Floyd's debut single was released. 'Arnold Layne' squirrelled its way up to number 20 in the charts, whilst the band squirrelled their way around the country gigging for all they were worth — often to four people and a dog who had no idea what they were listening to but didn't like it anyway, resulting in a split head from a tossed coin for Roger Waters one night.

The sight of Floyd hastily climbing the ladder to fame led to accusations from the drug-fuelled subculture inhabited by their fans that they were selling out. But Floyd had no intention of becoming victims of illicit substances à la Keith Richards. The scene had been a stepping stone for them on the road to success; they viewed it as a backdrop in front of which others could do as they pleased but not as integral to their own lives or music or indicative of their own philosophy towards the world. They did not want attachment to an underground movement that might subvert their musical careers.

However, the *"sheer madness"* of hurtling around Britain, together with the use of LSD and dope — although how much drug use was involved is still in contention — was having an adverse affect on Floyd's lead singer, the most artistically sensitive of the group, whose mind set placed him on a level apart from the others in the band. Whether or not Syd was taking acid everyday, his bandmates were concerned about him and the *"heavy, loony, messianic acid freaks"*, to quote Peter Jenner, who were his friends.

They had reason to be concerned, especially as they were embarking on their debut album at EMI's Abbey Road Studios. It was January 1967, and whilst the Beatles were in the adjacent studio 2 creating 'Sgt. Peppers Lonely Hearts Club Band*', producer and A&R executive Norman Smith was*

charged with helping Pink Floyd give birth to "The Piper at the Gates of Dawn", named after one of the chapters in Kenneth Grahame's 'The Wind in the Willows'.

Syd's intake of acid and his dislike of being told what to do with his music led to him ignoring all advice from Norman Smith. But both Syd and Roger were interested in the workings of the studio and the production of sound, and Syd proved to be a dab hand at the feeders on the desk, working them to get exactly the sound that he wanted.

Floyd steered themselves through loud — even the engineer was staggered by the decibel level — potential chaos to produce eleven tracks, six of which were written by Barrett alone, two by Barrett and Wright, one by Roger Waters and Barrett and one by Roger Waters alone. They also produced 'See Emily Play' as a single, also written by Syd Barrett. This single gave Norman Smith his **"aha!"** moment.

But who could have known that with the band on the outskirts of superstardom, Piper would be the only album with Syd Barrett fronting the band. David Gilmour, perhaps, who had a frightening experience when he met a **"… strange, glassy-eyed"** Syd one day.

Whilst Emily was released to the world on 16th of June 1967 and began working her way up the charts to number five with her psychedelic rock-pop charms, and Syd was just laid back enough not to frighten off the listening teenagers, the band were invited to appear on BBC TVs Top of the Pops.

Syd's problems became apparent almost immediately; he was unhappy at being told to mime the song and deliberately appeared in a dishevelled state, whereas the others had taken great care with their looks.

For his second TV appearance, Syd stood in front of the microphone with the guitar dangling in front of him and everyone knew what the problem was; as one friend described it, **"He looked completely off his head"**. Floyd's lead singer, it seemed, was having difficulties weaning himself from the idyllic days of his Cambridge childhood and was completely

incapable of coping with the hard-nosed adult world he found himself in. With hindsight, this is evident in the songs that he wrote for the album, which are infused with innocent wistfulness.

Syd's behaviour didn't frighten the BBC, apparently, who invited the group to return again for a radio show; but Syd had other ideas — maybe 'objections' would be a better word — and wasn't interested in appearing. So he didn't. The other members of the group, on the other hand, acutely aware that their lead singer's actions were likely to crash-land their nascent careers, weren't interested in putting up with Syd's erratic behaviour if it was going to cause the cancellation of Pink Floyd gigs, and they began to shun his company if possible.

By now, the Piper at the Gates of Dawn had been sent out into the world. It wasn't going to win over mainstream pop fans, but it did garner favourable reviews in the NME, which gave the album four stars out of five. It was described as **"a fine showcase for both their talent and their recording technique"**, with **"plenty of mind-blowing sound"** and **"a particularly striking collection"**. It has since been acknowledged as a seminal 1960's psychedelic rock album. Listeners would have been hard-pressed to find any blues in the album, though; Richard Wright's keyboard had superimposed jazz and classical ideas and taken over the interludes normally reserved for a slick lead guitar. The result was a musical silt-bed of menace beneath the spacey musical lines, howls and sound effects.

Floyd were now beginning to make inroads into the consciousness of the musical cognoscenti, and EMI were looking for another single from them. The texts of all of the songs on offer seemed to be doorways into Syd's mind, the mind of a man in the grip of **"…serious mental disturbance"**, in the words of Jenner. The band was so worried that they managed to get him a psychiatrist, an effort that came to nothing.

The tour to promote the album did nothing to allay anyone's ragged nerves. Floyd's work visas didn't arrive on time, and when they did get to the States their US label, Capitol, had left them without any instruments. Neither was opening for a raucous Janis Joplin the best of plans, their appearance drawing forth remarks from critics that their work was **"simply dull"**. And

22

MAIN IMAGE: London Roundhouse, Pink Floyd perform
with psychedelic light show projection, 15th October 1966

23

24

25

MAIN IMAGE: A psychedelic light show surrounds Pink Floyd playing
at the UFO Club, London, 23rd December 1966

Syd's unreliable behaviour continued as he smeared gel into his hair or detuned his guitar, gave monosyllabic answers in interviews and otherwise retreated into his own world.

Despite *"prodigious"* quantities of dope and being initiated into the delights of Joplin's crazy world, all in all, the band were left feeling disheartened and abandoned, so Andrew King killed the tour and took Floyd back home.

Clearly, Floyd could not continue with Syd in his current state, and Waters, for one, was angry enough about the *"Syd problem"* to want Barrett summarily dismissed. This, too, would have caused problems, as the band was due to go out on tour supporting Jimi Hendrix. In the event, Syd went with them bringing his pet problems along as well — arriving at the venue minutes before the band was due to play; sitting slumped in the dressing rooms seemingly petrified by any form of communication; and frequent acid trips did nothing to help the situation.

Syd, it seemed, could not reconcile his bandmates' desire for success and his own belief in art for art's sake. He knew his own shortcomings, knew that he was no Eric Clapton Mark II and was buckling under the pressure to become a superstar, lead singer-songwriter-come guru to Floyd's fans. But there was pressure on him backstage, too, to produce more songs for another single, especially as Blackhill were experiencing financial problems and going into debt, bouncing cheques and underpaying national insurance contributions. Syd could not have cared less about all of this, but the songs he produced were underwhelming. Floyd and their management were becoming extremely nervous about what was going to happen next. Gone the optimism from the summer of love; Floyd were in danger of imploding.

1967 drew to a close, and everyone who watched them could see that something bizarre was going on, even though the nature of Floyd's music might have papered over some of the performance cracks. One man who watched their gig at the Royal College of Art in London just thought that they were *"awfully bad"*. When people were talking about Syd, the word *"strange"* cropped up time and again. Even on stage, Barrett seemed to be disengaged with what was going on around him,

his eyes becoming duller, his face more pale by the day.

Mason knew that man in the audience at the Royal College of Art. It was David Gilmour. Letting the cat out of the bag, Mason asked him straight out if he would be interested in playing with Floyd should the need arise. But in a round about way, Gilmour would soon be left in no doubt by the other members of the group that they all wanted to see the back of Syd.

Even in his bombed-out state, Syd would have realised what was happening when Gilmour was invited to show what he could do at the Abbey Road Studios. There can be little doubt that he was afraid of Gilmour's guitar skills and saw him as a potential usurper. But the others in the band were in no mood to carry on as before. So, for a promised £30 a week, Gilmour was brought on board to cover up for the band's blatantly self-destructing front man.

The tension emanating from Barrett towards Gilmour was evident onstage, where Barrett became fixated by the new guitarist, circling him like a vulture. Neither did Gilmour's presence solve the problems within the group since Waters turned his difficult behaviour in the new man's direction, too. The management didn't put much faith in a Gilmour uncertain of himself, and thought that Wright and Barrett were the musical heart and soul of the group. They even considered hiving them off from Floyd to create another band. Either that or they would further his career as a solo artist.

And when they happened, the changes happened quickly.

In January 1968, the group simply decided they would not pick up Syd for a gig in Southampton. The now famous phrase *"Let's not bother"* was spoken. The genie was out of the bottle.

They came to the same decision for the next gig.

Finally, in March 1968, Jenner and King terminated their partnership with the group — and Bryan Morrison moved into the vacuum. Floyd now had a new manager; Steve O'Rourke, 27 years old and uncompromising in his dedication to the band.

27

28

MAIN IMAGE: L-R: Roger Waters, Nick Mason, Syd Barrett, Rick Wright group shot, at mixing desk in recording studio control room, 1967

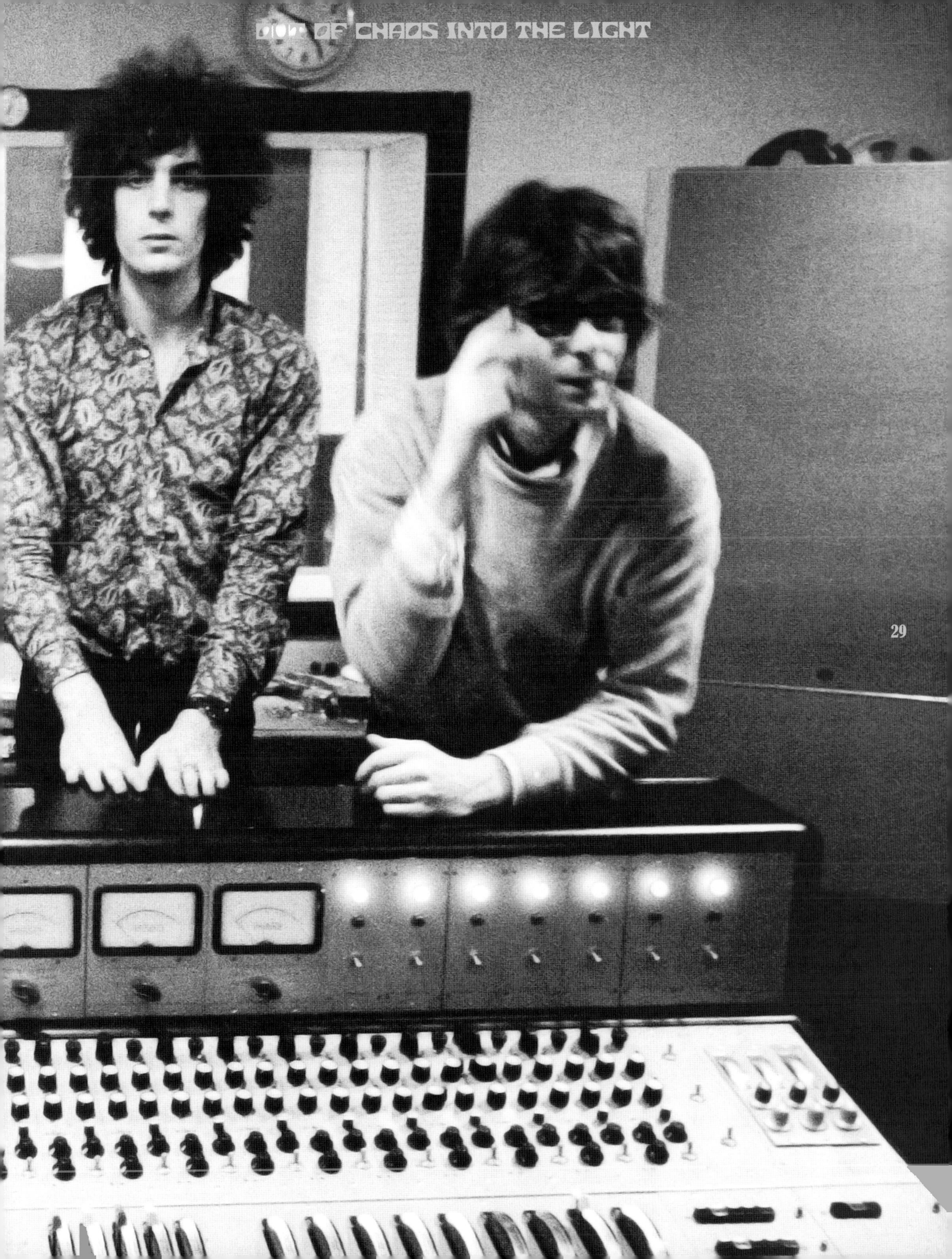

He immediately took matters in hand.

Syd's official departure from the band was announced on April the 6th. The end of a career that could have sparkled for years, crash-landed because of the fault lines in Barrett's character. The young man who had been extroverted and friendly had descended into memory lapses, incoherent speech patterns and mood swings, scaring his friends with blank, staring eyes. Fatally, he was now incapable of forming coherent musical connections.

Following on the heels of the rejection by Floyd, Barrett floated away into professional no man's land. He was still with girlfriend Lindsay but had now added aggression to his list of unpleasant characteristics. This was often directed at his girlfriend and they had furious rows, but he was also known to attack his friends physically. All those around him were dropping acid and smoking dope, there were groupies constantly searching for him and he seemed completely incapable of normal communication. Roger Waters later tried to get him to see the famed psychiatrist R. D. Laing. To no avail. But Jenner, King and the group tried to help in various ways, feeding him, keeping an eye on him, never turning him away wherever he turned up.

No one in the group had wanted this to happen and it had happened too fast for David Gilmour to be truly sown into the fabric of Floyd. So for the months ahead, Barrett and Wright would mime the songs on TV and otherwise try to fill in for the absent Barrett. As time went on, however, it became clear that Gilmour was not only a better guitar player than Barrett but a better singer, too. The proof of the pudding would come with the second album, now demanded by EMI, which would be without Barrett's talented songwriting abilities.

The band recorded from August 1967 until May 1968. It's unclear how much of Barrett ghosted around on the album that came to be called a Saucerful of Secrets. It's his voice singing 'Jugband Blues' and his guitar can, apparently, be heard on 'Remember a Day' and a few other tracks. Otherwise the singing belongs to all the other band members, with Waters contributing three songs, Wright composing and Waters, Wright, Gilmour — still, for the time being sensing himself to be an outsider, writing little and unable to use his skills in harmonic vocalisation — and Mason

co-composers on the title track. That title track, full of bundled sound, was Waters now pushing the experimental boundaries out even further. The result, according to AllMusic, was **"... dark and repetitive pulses".**

But despite some generally lukewarm reviews when the album was released on the 29th of June 1968, it climbed to number nine in the UK charts, although it was the only Pink Floyd album not to reach the charts in the US. It contained what became a standard for the group far into the future; Roger Waters' 'Set the Controls for the Heart of the Sun', one of the tracks on which Barrett's guitar effects can be heard. Its cover graphics were the first by the band's Cambridge pals Storm Thorgerson and Aubrey 'Po' Powell, who called themselves Hipgnosis.

Floyd took off on another American tour testing their new lineup. And it was a humiliating repeat of the first tour, as they were made to feel like second-rate performers amongst American bands and left to idle their lives away in cheap motels before running out of money completely.

Waters was now the driving force of the band and seemed to feel that he needed to inherit some of Syd's strange behaviour, whilst David Gilmour had to find the strength of character to withstand Waters' strong personality and create a persona that would edge out the shadow of Syd. **"I know I can be an oppressive personality because I bubble with ideas and schemes"**, Waters said of himself, maintaining that he had assumed leadership of the band because nobody else seemed interested in doing so.

Restarting Floyd's flight path after Syd's departure was not helped by the release of the single 'Point Me at the Sky', an unfortunate choice that proved the group's inability to write hit singles. Written by Gilmour and Waters, it failed to chart in the UK. But it was on the B-side, 'Careful with That Axe Eugene', that the seeds of Floyd's future could be observed quietly germinating. Here was Floyd veering far off into abstraction, shunning the pop-song straitjacket and embracing the effects of sound. Music to mellow by, par excellence.

PERFECT FOR THE AGE INTO WHICH IT WAS BORN.

30

31

WEIRD NONSENSE

In 1969, Floyd went into the studios to record the soundtrack for the film 'More' by Barbet Schroeder, a left-wing French film director. They were happy to do so, not only for the financial benefits but also because they understood that their style of playing lent itself to soundtracks, and that film music might be a way forward if all else failed. Waters rolled his sleeves up with gusto, and although the film vanished, the soundtrack zipped smartly into the top 10.

32

Also in 1969, Syd Barrett returned to music for a short solo career spanning two years. Initially, although his ideas were good, he seemed incapable of pulling a song together, on occasion incapable of even standing up or holding his plectrum. Nevertheless, David Gilmour, who still stayed in close contact with Barrett, and Roger Waters stepped in to try and rescue the project. The Madcap Laughs was released on the 3rd of January 1970. Suffice it to say that EMI, who had wanted to shut down the project anyway, did not bother about asking for a second album from the wayward singer. They had had enough of *"Weird nonsense"* as they called Floyd's music on the More soundtrack. The Madcap Laughs album included many mistakes made during recording, for which Waters and Gilmour were criticised. However, at the time, it seemed to the two guitarists that their main task was to try and give Syd a wake-up call and pull him back from the edge.

Their efforts went unrewarded.

Syd's life this year took another turn for the worse; he lived in a darkened room that was descending into the pit with him, and he started a complicated relationship with a gorgeous new girlfriend, Gala Pinion, which involved physical violence and extreme changes in mood that could see him turn from ork to angel within seconds. But he was just as likely to remain silent for hours on end. No one really felt that his behaviour was particularly out of the ordinary in an atmosphere where drug taking, and at the time, Mandrax (Quaalude), especially, was almost mandatory for anyone wanting to be accepted as part of the in-crowd.

Except that Syd's drug taking was already excessive.

Nevertheless, in that same year there were good vibrations for Wright and Waters, and for Mason, too. They all got married; Wright to Juliette Gale, Waters to Judy Trim and Mason to Lindy Rutter.

At the same time as these events were taking place, and in between gigs around the country, the band were recording their third album, a double album released on the 25th of October 1969; Ummagumma. With no clear idea of what they were going to do in the studio, the band added two solo pieces from Waters and one each from the others to complement live recordings of 'Astronomy Domine' and 'Careful with That Axe Eugene', together with 'Set the

RIGHT: Pink Floyd shrouded in pink with new member Dave Gilmour, back right, August 1968

WEIRD NONSENSE

Controls for the Heart of the Sun' and 'A Saucerful of Secrets'. Waters used vocal and percussion effects whilst Wright was the Lord of Darkness on a variety of keyboards. It might have seemed an inconspicuous birth, but the five musicians had come a long way; so far, indeed, that the Record Mirror claimed Ummagumma to be *"a truly progressive rock album"*. Other reviews were equally favourable, although the band themselves were less enthusiastic calling it *"A failed experiment"* or simply *"horrible"*, to quote Gilmour, with Richard Wright calling his own contribution *"pretentious"*. They sensed that their live improvisation style did not translate well onto tape in the studio. The fans didn't agree and the 86.21 minutes of Ummagumma were raised into the UK top five.

The mood in the band wasn't raised when their next project, the soundtrack for a film by director Michelangelo Antonioni, turned into a sheer slog and they watched the film vanish into the ether.

Scottish composer, poet and musician Ron Geesin had become friends with Nick and Lindy Mason and, by osmosis, the rest of the band, and towards the end of 1969, Geesin and Waters got together to produce a soundtrack to a documentary; The Body.

Geesin was soon to figure even more prominently in the life of the band.

Early in 1970, the men at EMI seemed to change their minds about weirdness after The Madcap Laughs clocked up sales of 5000 copies in two months. Syd, who was, at least, painting, even if he didn't finish anything he started, seemed to be deeply aware, and disturbed, about what had happened to him, the *"… failed pop star"*, as he called himself in his lucid moments.

Wright and Gilmour, despite often being out on the road with Floyd thanks to gigs booked by Bryan Morrison in Europe and the UK, including every university they could get to, stepped in to help out again, showing how much they cared about the fate of their erstwhile bandmate. Which was

just as well, because Syd was in a weird state oscillating between lost and found whilst ignoring all suggestions. His friends realised it would be a question of taking what came and hoping that something usable would emerge at the end.

Syd's dislocated behaviour continued to worry all those around him. Friends remarked that driving in a car with him was extremely scary, because he could simply lose concentration entirely or just stop the car wherever it was and get out. At any rate, he was already beyond the reach of mere mortals.

Gala stayed with him loyally and went to Cambridge with him when he moved back in with his mother.

The next news to shock Syd's friends was that the two were engaged. Syd was now going to study medicine.

Then the engagement was off.

It wouldn't be too long before Gala was off, too.

As with Syd, EMI had undergone a change of heart about Floyd, too, cheered by the sales of their previous album. So Waters, after the recent experience of working with Ron Geesin, asked him to participate in the next album.

Seeing the Floyd close-up for the first time, Geesin observed the *"easy-going"* Wright and Mason and the reserved but stubborn when he felt that he needed to be Dave Gilmour. It was obvious that Roger, was an overbearing personality, extremely difficult to get along with, frightening, even, but the creative powerhouse, the *"ideas man"* of the group. Geesin and Waters became good friends until the time Waters scythed down almost everyone in his vicinity. The fluctuating alliances within the group were draining, more so for Rick Wright, perhaps, who had been seen as the group's pretender to the songwriting throne left vacant by Barrett, but which had been usurped by Waters. The antagonism between the two would continue unabated. Waters, Geesin

remembers, spent most of his time moaning about the others and their inability to manifest his ideas. Nonetheless, he would leave the group only when he finally felt financially secure. Wisely, aware of the conveyor-belt nature of the conflicts amongst them, the group tried to contain it all within a Floydian bubble until such time as they could face the world united behind an album or a concept.

Their inability to gel personally had been highlighted during a trip to France in August, where they had gone to write some music for the French choreographer Roland Pettit. The band and their wives all resided in a large villa, which led to clashes between Waters and Mason and the band members' wives, who were all strong women in their own right. Tensions followed them outside of the villa, leading to cancelled performances and the group eventually flying home. The music would see the light of performance in 1972 for shows in Marseille and Paris.

By October 1970 the album was ready, and it hit the streets on October the 2nd. Atom Heart Mother was a collection of tracks that the band had put together before they asked Geesin to complete the whole with an orchestral arrangement whilst they went off on tour in the US. Geesin took away the various ideas, whilst trying to wrestle with the backing tape that EMI had insisted be recorded in one take, a technique that resulted in inconsistencies in the tempo. Geesin added choirs and brass, but when he came to conduct the session musicians, their perceived lack of initiative and the clash of style almost led to fisticuffs, and the Scotsman had to be replaced.

Whatever agonies its birth caused, Atom Heart Mother (a title attached to the album when the band found an article about a woman given a nuclear-powered pacemaker, but which had nothing to do with the music — up until then the album had been blessed with the title 'The Amazing Pudding') flew up to number one in the UK, a first for Floyd, and number 55 in the US; in Holland, France and Germany it floated into the top 10.

Nevertheless, the critics were divided about its value,

and it was either *"Utterly fantastic"* or *"Folk at its deadly worst"*, and the band, too, was unhappy with the results with Gilmour quoted as saying that they were scraping the barrel a bit at that period as though they hadn't got one decent idea between them. But the fans didn't seem to mind that they wandered between English whimsy, Floydian breakfast-time sound effects, ethereal brain-feathering and nostalgic self-exploration. And the ambivalence of the album's reception was tempered for the band by the fact that now, finally, they were earning more than their road crew.

On tour through the United States that year, the album received a similar divergence in reception with Leonard Bernstein singularly unimpressed but Stanley Kubrick wanting some of the music for his film A Clockwork Orange.

So the band entered the 70s in relatively good shape.

Syd Barrett not quite so.

Before the end of the year 1971, his second solo album had appeared. With the title of simply Barrett, it failed to chart either in the UK or in the US. It was a difficult birth, as Barrett never played the same thing twice or in the same way, and his airy-fairy statements that the music was too *"windy"* or *"afternoon-ish"* didn't help one bit.

In the meantime Floyd were busy.

In 1971, they went on tour in Australia, which led to another project; they wrote the twenty-three minute 'Echoes' for the surfer and film director George Greenough as a soundtrack for his documentary about surfing. Echoes proved to be a huge stepping stone in the evolution of Floyd's music; after many years of striding through the musical jungle, they had come to a crossroads; as David Gilmour said, *"... we found our focus"*.

Anyone who was in the studio with them in 1971 might have begged to differ with that opinion. The band worked on the project, now referred to as the Household Objects album,

37

for a long time, experimenting, it comes as no surprise, with household objects such as wine glasses, aerosol cans or cigarette lighters. Their efforts were then consigned to *"the rubbish library"*, as Gilmour dubbed it, although retrieved in later years. Nonetheless, their record company, EMI, continued to indulge them in their musical meanderings, of which the Household Objects album was neither the first nor the last.

'Echoes' proved surprisingly cohesive and determinedly melodic despite its piecemeal birth. As usual, Gilmour and

Waters were in the driving seat. Waters professed to be bored with most of Floyd's material and Echoes was an attempt to shake off the tag *"space rock band"* that they had carried around with them since the beginning and which they so despised. His admiration for the Plastic Ono Band album led to his attempt to instill a sense of sharp reality into his writing. He referenced his sense of alienation in his early London years and the period after Barrett's sad exit.

Progress was being made, however, and once the group had honed the various disconnected bits of ideas on stage

39

during their gigs, 'Echoes' would find its way onto their next album. The project working title started off inconspicuously as 'Nothings', a series of, as yet, unconnected experiments in sound in the studio. Before too long, 'Son of Nothings' emerged, to be superseded by 'Return of the Son of Nothings'. The band were recording in between performing throughout Britain and Europe, so the recording of the new album took some considerable time, spread between January and August 1971 and involving several recording studios all over Britain.

On tour, where Water's desire for spectacle conflicted with the instincts of Wright and Gilmour, the band filled the hours of bone-numbing boredom with mahjong or Monopoly. If the band is to be believed, groupies were not on the menu to anything like the extent indulged in by their fellow rock bands. Neither did their behaviour offstage come close to paralleling that of their famous rivals in Led Zeppelin or the Stones. Indeed, when not touring they had embraced bourgeois lifestyles in permanent homes. Even confirmed bachelor David Gilmour was living in a farmhouse in Essex by the end of the year. Perhaps his meeting with 21-year-

40

PINKFLOYD A Kaleidoscope of Conundrums

MAIN IMAGE: Pink Floyd gig on 16th June 1971 at the abbey of Royaumont

41

42

old Philadelphian model Virginia "Ginger" Hasenbein had nudged him in the direction of domesticity. Gilmour met her in Michigan in October 1971; love at first sight, as Ginger said later. Within two weeks, she had given up everything in America to go and live in England. They would marry in 1975, finally divorcing in 1990, four children later.

The band had composed five new pieces for side one of the new album, two of which, 'A Pillow of Winds' and 'Fearless', were composed by Waters and Gilmour alone with Waters composing and singing 'St Tropez' by himself. Only the track, 'One of These Days' could be accused of being even remotely 'space rock'. The group effort 'Seamus', managed to top the polls as the band's worst song ever and

On the 31st of October 1971, its working title now abandoned, 'Meddle' arrived in the shops and to a very favourable critical response. It wended its way up to number 3 in the United Kingdom and number 2 in Holland, faring less well in the United States where it became a victim of poor publicity. *"An exceptionally good album",* drooled the NME; *"Another masterpiece by a masterful group"*, according to another critic. David Gilmour was praised for being *"a real shaping force in the group"*. Floyd, it seems, had changed tack and most of the world liked what it heard.

APART FROM THOSE WHO THOUGHT THAT THE VOCALS WERE DRIPPY AND THE INSTRUMENTALS

43

THE LAZIEST GROUP EVER

Oddly enough, for what Gilmour described as basically "the laziest group ever", Meddle was not Pink Floyd's only album in 1971. Relics had been released in May that year. This, however, was not due to more hard work by the band, but rather because the men from EMI were worried that Meddle would take a long time to finish thus leaving a large gap between Atom Heart Mother and the new album. So they put together a compilation of eleven tracks including several by Syd Barrett and a previously unreleased song by Roger Waters, 'Biding My Time'. The album worked its way up to number 32 in the United Kingdom achieving gold certification.

Floyd also became involved in a project that was filmed in Pompeii, a rock movie that fired the band's imagination. So, in October, they found themselves in Pompeii playing 'A Saucerful of Secrets' in the roasting Mediterranean sun with Mount Vesuvius as a backdrop. They spent four days filming, with just the director Adrian Maben and the crew as their audience in the vast amphitheatre. They topped this off with studio shots in Paris in December.

All this, plus a tour of Britain, Japan and the United States in December.

Although reluctant to be involved with his former bandmates, Syd fluttered around on the periphery of their existence. And he was playing gigs with the musician called Jack Monck in a group they called Stars. They played small gigs in 1972 but it took no time at all before Barrett was reduced to a familiar musical incoherence on stage that had people in the audience who knew him, close to tears. Aware of his own incompetence and his mental predicament, Barrett would then vent his anger on furniture — and his own head.

Floyd returned to Abbey Road Studios in June 1972 to start the recording sessions for a new album, which they would not complete until January 1973. They had developed and tried out the music they had composed for this album, which was to be called 'The Dark Side of the Moon', in live performances. One live show in January 1972 was a minor disaster, with taped sound effects refusing to obey and equipment ignoring the musicians. Gilmour and Waters walked off stage. An ominous start.

It had been Waters idea for a concept album with a unified single theme revolving around the pressures of living and the cause and effects of anxiety and madness. No prizes for guessing who was in his mind at the time. There would be no more lyrical beating about the bush as far as Waters was concerned; the songs would be direct, the meaning crystal clear. He always felt that he was the Don Quixote of realism, battling against the windmill arms of Syd's whimsy that floated around the other band members. He was determined that his political and philosophical interests would be given priority this time round.

44

RIGHT: Pink Floyd photo session in the Japanese garden, Tokyo, March 1972

This would be the first time that Roger Waters would write all the lyrics on an album, although the other members of the band were co-writers. Gilmour, however, later blamed himself for being lazy when he referred to the sparseness of his contributions to the lyric content, with his name on four of the songs, although his musical dominance on guitar and vocals is unquestioned.

The four band members, with help from those around them in the studio, put together a list of anything that was a cause for concern in their lives from violence to boredom and growing old, to create 'The Dark Side of the Moon'. Music came in hesitantly, with fragments from the past revisited and revitalised and new ones brought in on home tapes. By February they were on a roll, writing, recording and performing more and more of the work in progress with audiences in Portsmouth treated to a largish chunk of the album. A state-of-the-art lighting rig lit the t-shirted band when they went for the jugular at the Rainbow Theatre in London. They wanted to present themselves at their best, musically and physically.

46

The Rainbow shows were sold out and a new Floyd sound surged out onto the musical scene. Just two numbers, included to sooth audience sensitivities, pointed to the past with a finger as wraith-like as Syd, spotted in the audience one night.

Waters had by now written an ending entitled 'Eclipse', a dramatic flourish to what would be a dramatic musical experience.

In the midst of all of this excitement, the film world called to them again and they decamped to Paris to record the soundtrack for La Vallée from Iranian-born French director Barbet Schroeder. This filmic voyage of self-discovery portraying a westerner discovering a more meaningful life, was accompanied by Floyd's music, which they fashioned into an album, Obscured by Clouds for their fourth foray into film music.

The sessions spread over two weeks and were swift and precise, free of the usual Floyd open-ended improvisations, and each track lasted less than six minutes. The band scored

MAIN IMAGE: L-R: backing singers, Dave Gilmour, Nick Mason, Roger Waters, Dick Parry, Rick Wright performing live onstage on 'Dark Side of the Moon' Tour

the music to the visual cues, always under time constraints, a labour that Gilmour, at least, seemed to thoroughly enjoy, with all the band members pitching in with ideas — and credited, too. The songs were well constructed despite the lack of time.

So, fans were to be treated to docile vocals and ruminative piano accompaniments that had cast off the British tinge that had been the band's calling card. Waters' 'Free Four' was allowed to break free as a single in the US, its dark themes notwithstanding, and did well enough to justify its liberty, whilst 'Wot's… Uh the Deal?' is considered to be one of the most underrated of Floyd's output.

'Obscured by Clouds' was released in June 1972 and tore its way up to no 6 in the UK and no 1 in France, certified Gold in 1997. It didn't get there through praise from the music critics.

Although many dyed-in-the-wool fans are disdainful of the album, it's now considered a treasure that acted as a warm up for Dark Side.

47

And the beat went on at Abbey Road for the new album, with engineer Alan Parsons witness to the band turning up and improvising around the themes they had already developed, Wright producing what the engineer considered the best thing he ever did; 'The Great Gig in the Sky', and Gilmour's guitar work on 'Time', outstanding.

By now summer was beckoning hard, and before taking off on tour in the US, the band took some time away from the studio, though not from themselves, vacationing together in Lindos, Greece.

The US had not been an easy nut for the band to crack up until then, but they set off on the fourteen-concert tour with their popularity on the increase thanks to Obscured by Clouds. They then hit the studio in the UK again with the addition of jazz musician Dick Parry on sax; although they had little time in London because Marseille was calling; in the form of a ballet. The Ballet de Marseilles, to be accurate, with whom they performed five shows in November.

Then it was finally time to put the album to bed; time to say goodbye to the multitrack recording, analog synthesisers and tape loops and to singer Claire Torry, which they did in January of 1973. Incidentally, Torry had been told to *"improvise"* and think about horror, but lacking any proper direction her performance embarrassed her. Needlessly, as it turned out, as she compressed all the elements of the album's themes into her superb, dramatic vocals. She felt even more embarrassed when no one said a word to her after her session was over; she had just come across the insular side of Pink Floyd, who, selfishly perhaps, never felt the need to communicate with anyone. This sentiment extended to the music press, to whom Floyd wished to remain enigmatic and therefore unavailable. According to David Gilmour, the band had come to understand that you didn't need to talk to the press to sell records; so they didn't. This, of course, did not really endear them to the fraternity of music journalists.

Floyd also bid farewell to the *"massive rows"*, arising from the passionate beliefs about the music, which had led to three separate mixes; to the arguments about a *"warmer sound"* wanted by Gilmour and Wright or the harder mix and dominant vocal segments that Waters and Mason preferred. The impasse was broken when the band brought in Chris Thomas to act as an arbitrator between the quarrelling members.

Just before the new album could be slipped into its iconic sleeve with the prism spectrum graphic designed by Storm Thorgeson — now one of the most famous covers in popular music history and one which beautifully reflected the album's themes — Waters had a final flash of inspiration and followed through on his idea to add speech fragments to the tracks, which would weave through the songs. Anyone and everyone who would answer questions was roped in to do so. It proved to be a scintillating idea.

The fans would be treated to a continuous piece of music on either side of the album five tracks, exploring five steps of human existence, moving through the stresses we are subjected to on our human journey, to the greed of life, the isolation, the conflict and, inevitably by now, the mental breakdown. 'Time' was a warning and a broadside at the rat race that could eat at a life filled with trivialities whilst time passed unnoticed, a track which tied into 'Money', on which the opening sounds of cash registers and clinking change make its mocking intent very clear. And then, of course, there were Waters' pet scenes of violence, death and fear expressed in 'Brain Damage', 'The Great Gig in the Sky' and 'Us and Them'. Waters' felt that Barrett's mother blamed him for her son's illness, for leading him into the drug dens of London, so it's hardly surprising that his thoughts and those of his fellow band members should continually return to Syd's collapsed life. The final sequence, 'Eclipse', with its rising gospel vocals introduces hope; not only hope for Syd and hope for themselves but for all humanity.

Sometimes, it's easier to be a theory guru than a practitioner on the ground; engineer Alan Parsons might have had reason to think so when his long hours, attention to detail and initiative brought in no more financial gain than his fee at the time for the recording. Despite his Grammy Award for his work.

48

MAIN IMAGE: Nick Mason of Pink Floyd performs on stage, London, 1972

49

Waters was convinced that the group had just produced something extremely special, and after the reviewers had listened to the band's work, he was proven right. The album went to number one in the US, Austria, Canada, and to number 2 in the UK, Australia, Holland and Norway. *"Grandeur", " Floyd's most artistic musical venture", "textural and conceptual richness"* were just some of the words of praise used by critics. There were others; *"kitsch masterpiece"*; 'The Great Gig in the Sky' should have been canned, suggested another. But The Dark Side of the Moon became one of the bestselling albums of all time; the eighth bestselling album of all time in the UK.

Waters' messages had risen to the surface and were understood by those who heard them; they throbbed in the rhythm of an era of financial bleakness in Britain and the sound of IRA bombs detonating.

The band escaped dour Britain in March when they set off on a short tour of America to promote the album, enjoying *"one of the best shows ever"* after rising up onto the stage at New York City's Radio City Music Hall.

After a short sojourn home with concerts in Britain, which included sold-out nights at Earls Court in London surrounded by dry ice and *"blinding lights"* but without Claire Torry — who later, sadly, had to sue the band for royalties — by June they were back across the Atlantic. They had reason to be optimistic and in high spirits; by April the album had gained gold certification in the US. Eager to raise the band's profile amongst American record buyers even more, the record company persuaded them to release one of the tracks as a single, something that the band never wanted to do. The track chosen was 'Money', and although the musicians *"didn't think anything would happen"*, according to Wright, the single gave them their first hit in the United States — albeit cut in length and with the word 'bullshit' removed — when it went to number 10 in Cash Box magazine and on the Billboard Hot 100 reached number 13, remaining on the Hot 100 chart for over 14 years.

The band spent part of their new-found wealth — their new record company Columbia Records had reportedly advanced them $1 million — on new houses; a country manor house near Cambridge for Wright, a new house in Highgate for Mason, and the lads added villas in Greece and in the south of France to their possessions.

With their 42 minutes 49 seconds of music sandwiched between heartbeats, Pink Floyd had soared to the top of the pile and was now flavour of the month. Floyd broke box office records at the Union City Roosevelt Stadium. New fans, drawn by the single they had heard on the radio, came to hear these new hippies in town, came to hear the single played live and dance; which somewhat nonplussed a group used to fans who would dreamily listen to their music whilst horizontal.

NO ONE COULD EVEN GUESS AT WHAT PINK FLOYD MIGHT LOOK LIKE FROM THERE ON IN.

MAIN IMAGE: Pink Floyd perform on stage at the Olympisch Stadion on 22nd May 1972 in Amsterdam, Netherlands

51

THE PAST IS STILL THE FUTURE

WISH YOU WERE HERE

Even the name conjures up the memories of things that used to be; the album itself would become Richard Wright's favourite, despite the problems in the studio during its conception at Abbey Road at the end of 1973, which led to Waters dubbing the album 'Wish You Weren't Here'. And even though Syd Barrett really wasn't there, Waters' seeming obsession with his former bandmate's persona permeates his lyrical direction.

Wish You Were Here started out life with the band listlessly messing around with household objects in the studio once again and producing nothing useable, except a finger run around the rim of a wineglass. They were suffering from exhaustion, physical and emotional; *"Rather badly mentally ill"*, as Waters described it slightly more graphically. Mason's marriage was collapsing and the general motivational malaise did not ease as 1973 turned into 1974, either. It was hard to keep the muse interested in a lifeless King's Cross rehearsal studio without windows.

As they turned into pop stars, Floyd became victims of another malaise that has led to the downfall of many celebrities; as Nick Mason said later, *"We seemed to be more interested in booking squash courts than perfecting the set"*. They even took to choosing their tour hotels according to their vicinity to a golf course.

In the studio, Waters slowly began to carve a creative direction for another album and brought some lyrics in for three new songs, which seemed to prove that the success of the Dark Side of the Moon had encouraged him to be even more vitriolic towards his pet hates. And that a phantom Syd was always sitting on his shoulder.

Gilmour had composed a four-note guitar phrase that reminded Waters of Syd, who, incidentally, would visit the studio unannounced in 1975. That phrase found its way into the song 'Shine On You Crazy Diamond' — along with Waters' lyrics, *"… when you were young you shone like the sun"* — as did the sound of the finger on the rim of the glass. Although Barrett talked a little during his visit, it was obvious to everyone that he was spiritually absent, and the dramatic change in his appearance was a deeply upsetting experience to Waters.

Three songs, 'Shine On You Crazy Diamond', 'Raving and Drooling' (later became 'Sheep') and 'You've Got to be Crazy' (later became 'Dogs') emerged from the sessions and were played on tour in France and in the UK in 1974. But although the latter two songs were intended for the new album they were eventually discarded to be used on different projects. Floyd played the songs in the first half of their shows, which

52

53

54

55

were now enhanced by a 40-foot circular screen for films and photos and the animations of filmmaker and cartoonist Gerald Scarfe, and followed them with The Dark Side of the Moon. Scarfe, with an outsider's objectivity, would also note the dynamics within the group; Mason's diplomacy and organisational role, Waters' leadership, Wright living in a bubble of his own, and the easy-going Gilmour, whose main focus of concern was for the music itself.

Their new show also sparkled in New York's Radio City Hall before hitting the UK in November, where 'Shine On' was often dedicated by Waters to Barrett, the absent musician whose legacy — often infused with guilt and fear — followed them.

With royalties coming in, Barrett moved back to London and took up residence in Sloane Square. The ex-Floyd member had acquired the image of a damaged romantic surrounded by tristesse and mystique, although David Gilmour was one of those who saw through the nostalgic veil and knew that something was *"drastically wrong"* with his former bandmate. Within a short space of time, Barrett had gone on a spending spree and was a frequent visitor to the local pub. He had become bloated, shaved his head, and was often seen wandering the streets in a variety of clothes ranging from Hawaiian shirts to women's dresses. Everyone who had known him remarked on the great changes to his personality.

Although EMI wanted another Barrett album and even managed to steer him into the studio to play whatever he wanted on whatever instrument he wanted, the sessions turned out to be catastrophic. There were no new songs. On one famous occasion they weren't even any guitar strings.

On tour, Richard Wright, for one, often felt dwarfed by Floyd's sets, for they were now dragging around with them mountains of sound and light equipment that needed to be handled by a veritable shoal of technicians and stagehands, who, nonetheless, could not prevent unreliable equipment from interrupting the shows; there were malfunctioning projectors, cues missed, failing sound systems. And a new

mixing desk also had a mind of it's own. All of this led to frayed tempers and technicians hired and fired. The strained atmosphere was coupled with a sense of unease about the new material and a suspicion that the music had somehow slipped into second place behind the spectacle.

That this mentality had seeped into their personal behaviour did not escape the critics, either, who accused them of disrespecting the audience with their cavalier attitude (and clothing, with Gilmour coming in for particular criticism in this respect) on stage. The sense that the adulation aimed at them was absurd, combined with the incongruity of seeing a performance that they perceived as being bad, praised to the hilt, made Waters and Gilmour realise that they had lost their way after The Dark Side and something needed to change. In fact, everyone was going through the ropes. According to Gilmour, it was a *"... confusing and sort of empty time for a while"*.

Each member of the group considered leaving as Floyd tumbled into 1975, with Mason suffering in particular because of his personal life and Waters becoming even angrier than usual. He was now dominating Floyd's lyrics, to the chagrin of Gilmour, and wanting another concept album driven by the idea of spiritual absence, whereas Gilmour longed for more musicality. Neither did all of the band members share Waters' overall cynical views on life.

In this fractured atmosphere filled with suspicion, Floyd pieced together the components of the new album, but without enthusiasm. On some days, nothing happened at all and on others they would play word games and get drunk. Painfully slowly, they began to extract the rabbit from its hole. They decided, Waters decided, not to make 'Shine on You Crazy Diamond' fill one side but to have it introduce and then end the album; they also decided to put aside 'Raving and Drooling' and 'Got to be Crazy' for use on another album. Instead, Waters penned 'Welcome to the Machine' and 'Have a Cigar' to replace them and co-wrote the title song with Gilmour. Although more upbeat than most of the material on the album, the song's reference to *"... two lost souls"*, the second lost soul possibly being his wife with whom his

MAIN IMAGE: Rick Wright performing on stage, 1974

relationship was disintegrating, touched again on physical presence and spiritual absence.

Indeed, the general thrust of the album's philosophy aligned well with Waters' view on life. He wrote in unflinchingly harsh terms about people searching for a dream all their lives only to find that it's hollow, that it doesn't transport you onto a higher personal plane of contentment. It was obvious where the fulcrum of his present discontent was centred. And unhappy that the flow of Syd's life had never been accurately captured in the press, he honed 'Shine On You Crazy Diamond' through several rewrites to reveal the essence of what he felt about Syd's sad withdrawal from life. Waters' preoccupation with his former bandmate's fate seemed to reflect a worry that he might somehow inadvertently stumble along the same path himself and that if he wrote about it he might be able to understand why, and therefore avoid his own crash-landing.

The sessions waded on through the year and into June, when the band were due to depart for the second US tour of that year following their initial American stint in April.

And then, on the 5th of June, a strange man appeared in the studio, overweight, his head and eyebrows shaven, holding a plastic bag and, as Mason remembered, wearing a decrepit old tan mackintosh. It was Syd Barrett. Mason didn't recognise him and Waters, shocked by Syd's physical decay, said later that he had been reduced to tears by the sight of his friend.

Memories of the events seem sketchy, with some of those present reporting that Syd turned up on subsequent days and that he even offered to play guitar. Some people thought that he had also turned up at the wedding meal after David Gilmour had married his girlfriend Ginger on July the 7th. It remained another of those poignant, tangential encounters marking Syd's decline.

It also remained the very final encounter, as none of the members of Floyd would ever see him again.

There was good reason to be satisfied with the US tour; it sold-out, with reports of 67,000 tickets sold in a single day. Fans were treated to the sight of an inflatable pyramid, which made it through to June the 20th before inverting itself and disappearing over the side of the stadium wall into a car park. In Ontario, spectators were fortunate not to lose their hearing when four sticks of dynamite blew out the venue's back wall and showered splinters of light bulb glass onto everyone below.

59

MAIN IMAGE: Pink Floyd on Stage in France, 1974

Their was more chaos, too, at the July the 5th Knebworth music festival gig, their last live performance until 1977, which included fluctuating power supply problems that sent Wright's keyboards out of tune.

As the recording sessions drew to a close, the idea for another iconic album cover surfaced; two men in suits shaking hands, one of them on fire. It was conceived by Storm Thorgerson and intended to imply physical contact and spiritual absence in keeping with the album's overall theme. Very apt, as Waters was soon to get divorced from his wife, and the draft of a book about Pink Floyd opened up the uncomfortable truth for David Gilmour — that Roger Waters was the de facto leader of the group.

The recording sessions ended in July and Wish You Were Here was released on the 12th of September 1975.

They had, in the opinion of many fans and critics, produced their magnum opus. The album found itself in the number one spot after advanced sales of 250,000 units. Within two weeks, it was number one on the US Billboard chart and became the fastest-selling album of all time.

The band were generally satisfied with their work; Mason later expressed surprise at the quality they had achieved, (despite his not receiving a writing credit for the first time ever), Gilmour thought it better then the previous album, and felt the same as Wright — who had songwriting credits on eight tracks and made his synthesisers, organ and piano powerful forces throughout — that it was their best album to date. Waters, on the other hand, thought it was musically underdeveloped. His doubts notwithstanding, he was glad that listeners had understood the sadness, the aura of disconnection and the emotional coldness of the record, a musical ambience that he had striven hard to achieve. It seemed to be a highly accurate amalgam of the elements of Floydian life in the mid 70s.

So what did the critics think at the time?

Reviews were, in fact, placed quite heavily towards one end of the spectrum; *"… passion is everything of which Pink Floyd is devoid": "… unconvincing in its ponderous sincerity": "… desperate, uninspired… recycling the more obvious musical bits of 'Moon'. And one that must have been particularly hurtful for Roger Waters: ".… a fumbled opportunity for Waters really to sing about Syd Barrett". But there was also "… concise, highly melodic and very well played" and "… symphonic dignity".* No matter; by 2015, Rolling Stone would be giving it the accolade of the fourth greatest progressive rock album.

What to do then, after yet another runaway success? What any self-respecting successful band would do; they bought a building and set up their own recording studio and storage space.

This they did in Islington in North London at 35 Britannia Row, where they could now house the mammoth quantity of audio and lighting gear they had acquired. Without any plans for touring in 1976, the band set about their next album in their new 24-track studio in April. They brought with them the old conflicts that were still writhing below the surface, and the world outside seem to reflect Roger Waters' own increasingly inflammatory mindset — even though he had a new love life in the shape of Carolyne Anne Christie; punk rock was polarising the music scene and spitting at the supergroups, of which Floyd was definitely one, and Pink Floyd began work in a record heat wave amid violence at the Notting Hill carnival.

61

Within the group, resentments arose at Roger *"really keeping Dave down"* and the lack of songwriting credits. This was important, because songwriting royalties were allocated on a composition basis. Waters' opening and closing the album with a late addition, 'Pigs on the Wing', which was split into two thus doubling his potential royalties, did not help matters. With neither Mason nor Wright bringing songs to the table and David Gilmour's attention directed towards his domestic life, Ginger having just given birth to their daughter Alice, this shift in the centre of gravity produced an ominous cloud that would soon balloon in size and deluge the parade.

MAIN IMAGE: Pink Floyd performing live onstage on Winter Tour, 1974

62

Inside this atmosphere of dissent and antagonism, Animals began to take shape. Four of the album's five tracks were written by Waters, who shared the co-writing honours on 'Dogs' with Gilmour. So it was once again a Roger Waters' concept, on this occasion inspired by George Orwell's Animal Farm, with the barbs aimed at capitalism not Stalinism. The book's central ideas were ripe for plucking by Waters, concerned as he was with prejudice, inequality, rapacious capitalism, the blunting of human compassion and the resultant moral decrepitude of the community of mankind. Hence society's classes are divided up into mindless and unquestioning sheep, despotic pigs and aggressive dogs, their depictions intended to reflect human behaviour and attitudes. 'Raving and Drooling' and 'You've Got to be Crazy', which hadn't made it onto Wish You Were Here, were re-fashioned and became 'Sheep' and 'Dogs'.

Gilmour may have been sidelined on the songwriting front, but his sole contribution as vocalist, in 'Dogs', was later described as *"explosive"*, and some of his best work, as he dived into the uncompromising, bitter sentiments that deal with money-oriented ladder climbers. 'Pigs on the Wing' parts 1 and 2 was another of Waters' contributions that came up on the outside lane at the last minute and was unusual Floyd fare; a pure love song, Waters being *"… in love"* with girlfriend Carolyne Anne Christie. This was the first time a pure love song had been accorded the privilege of being on a Floyd album. Whilst Animals was being recorded, in November 1976 Caroline gave birth to little boy that she and Roger called Harry.

So the 41 minutes 41 seconds of Animals were completed by the end of the year, and the band turned its attention to the album's cover. A variety of ideas were rejected until Waters thought of floating an inflatable pig up amongst the chimney stacks of the deserted desolation of Battersea Power Station. The pig was intended as *"… a symbol of hope"*, said Waters, and another iconic Floyd album cover was about to be set free onto an unsuspecting public. What was also set free on the day of the photo shoot was the helium-filled pig, which broke its moorings and floated off southwards over Kent causing pandemonium at Heathrow's air traffic control,

until it landed in a farmer's field. Floyd and inflatable objects were not good news. The final cover was, in fact, a mixture of the dramatic cloud formations from the first day and a shot of sky-high 'Algie' the pig from the third day's shoot.

Amongst this unbearable excitement in December, Capital Radio listeners were treated to the first in a six-part series entitled 'The Pink Floyd Story', a coup for the broadcaster, which had netted interviews with a band notoriously reluctant to connect with the media.

On January the 23rd 1977, Animals was released.

To everyone's delight and Gilmour's surprise, it emulated the high-up-in-the-sky inflatable pig, reaching number 2 in the UK and number 3 in the US. It's worth taking a quote from the NME review; *"… one of the most extreme, relentless, harrowing and downright iconoclastic hunks of music to have been made available this side of the sun"*. Another review, damning with faint praise, said it was *"… a piece of well-constructed political program music"*.

So not everyone felt as affected as NME, and if Floyd had read the reviews they would also have seen the words *"pointless and tedious"*.

Waters described the album as violence tempered with sadness, and he must have been pleased when Melody Maker's Karl Dallas hit the nail on the head by saying that the album brought with it an *"… uncomfortable taste of reality in a medium that has become in recent years increasingly soporific"*.

So Animals was a different type of album, but Floyd were happy to be different, certainly happy trying to slip out from under the derogatory label *"Dinosaur Rock"* that they and their contemporaries were having hung around their necks, and they took their differentness out on tour, the In the Flesh Tour, across Europe, Britain, North America and Canada. The shows suffered from lack of rehearsal time, which meant that the performances were not uniformly good. Undaunted by their previous battles with helium, the pig went on tour with

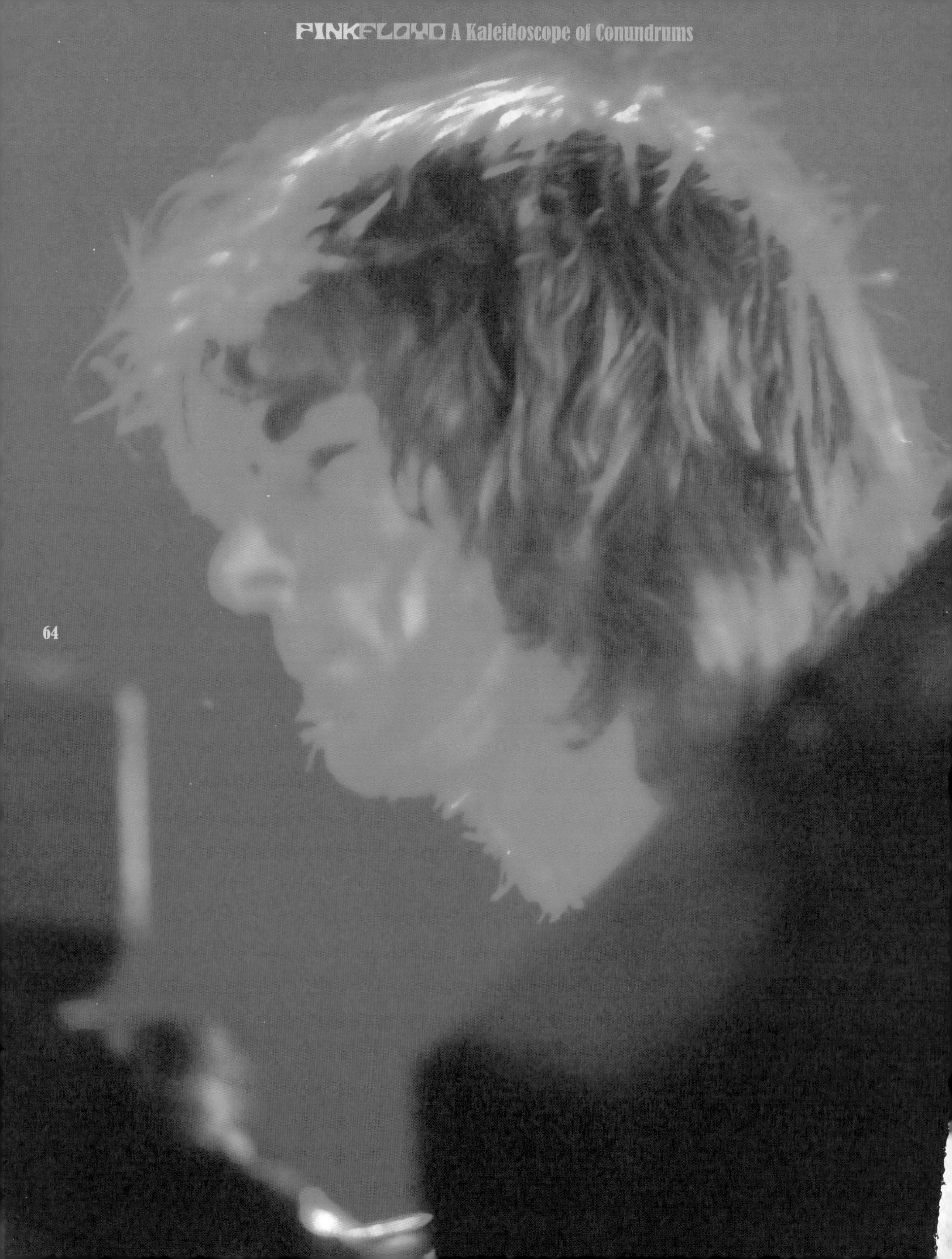

them and was joined by a helium-inflated family with a mother and father and their 2.4 children. US fans were subjected to even more neck-straining props in the form of an inflatable TV, a refrigerator and a car. Gerald Scarfe once again went to work on the animations, which matched the lyrics in their ruthlessness.

Floating in clouds of dry ice, which even obscured them from the audience, Pink Floyd seemed to have become victims of their own megalomania, and the sense that the music was being overwhelmed was now widespread. Neither did it help when audiences were overwhelmed with drugs and booze as they waited hours for the band to start playing. And what was almost worse, the headphones that the band were forced to wear to keep themselves synchronised with flying pigs and dry ice meant that they rarely had eye contact either with themselves or with their paying audience.

This on-stage disconnection seemed to be paralleled and fed by the group's off-stage internal tensions. Decay had set in, and the effects were becoming more and more visible, especially in Roger Waters, who had changed chameleon-like as soon as his life included the aristocratic Carolyne. Neither did the group's two influential wives, Carolyne and Gilmour's wife Ginger, see eye to eye, which resulted in more conflict and back-biting to add to the pressures already blighting the musicians' relationships.

Wright was becoming increasingly resentful of what he saw as Roger Waters' hypocrisy in railing against money and the establishment whilst wallowing in both, then isolating himself from the others whilst on tour and spending his time on local golf courses. At one point, the keyboard player took off back to England threatening never to return and had to be persuaded by their manager, Steve O'Rourke to come back.

Waters himself was spiralling into ever darker moods. The vast auditoria that swallowed both band and audience, audiences less interested in the subtleties of Floyd's music than in alcoholic, stoned partying, caused him intense frustration. He *"… loathed playing in stadiums"*, he complained, but the attitude of the others — with takings of $4 million for one gig — was that the gentleman doth complain too much. Waters' anger continued to seeth just below the surface, and when his love song to Carolyne, 'Pigs on the Wing', was accompanied by exploding fireworks from the audience one night, his temper also skyrocketed. *"You stupid motherfucker! Just fuck off and let us get on with it!"* he yelled at the audience.

None of this was good for his health. Before a show in Philadelphia, he was felled by stomach cramps and only able to go on to perform when a medic gave him an injection of muscle relaxant. He was later diagnosed with hepatitis. With numbed fingers, he walked on stage. At least he got the idea for another Floyd song 'Comfortably Numb' from the experience.

There were similar disturbances on the band's final performance in Montréal. An infuriated Roger Waters walked to the edge of the stage and spat in the face of an insistently loud fan.

Gilmour refused to join in the final encore of the six-month tour, and from the sound desk he watched his fellow band members perform, mulling over in his head the idea that perhaps Pink Floyd had reached the end of the road.

IN A CERTAIN SENSE THEY HAD.

65

MAIN IMAGE: Rick Wright of Pink Floyd performing on stage at Wembley Arena, London, 16th March 1977

THE WRIGHT MOMENT

1978 proved to be a year of wrenching change and anxiety for Pink Floyd.

In the hiatus at the end of the 'In the Flesh Tour' to promote the Animals album, when there was uncertainty about whether the band would ever make another album, all the Floyd members looked to projects outside of the band to expand their creative talents. Egged on by their wives, both Wright and Gilmour, who was also producing albums for Kate Bush and Unicorn, began work on solo albums. Gilmour's, entitled simply, David Gilmour, was born from his need to "… step out from behind Pink Floyd's shadow", and arrived on the streets first, on the 25th of May 1978 rising to number 17 in the UK. Wright's album, Wet Dream, caused barely a ripple when it was released in September 1978, but it was important for the keyboard player because even though he felt it was amateurish and the lyrics were somewhat lacking in character, in his own words, it "… helped me get back my creative energies".

Roger Waters had not been idle during this time, either, and Waters had produced enough demo material for two more albums, fortunately, for Pink Floyd, as it turned out, whatever gripes the others might have had about Waters hogging the songwriting limelight — apart from Wright, who kept all of his songs to himself anyway.

Mason, meanwhile, had been productive in a producer role on the album Green by former Gong guitarist Steve Hillage.

When Floyd reconvened at Britannia Row in July, Waters' demos were played to the others, and the set of compositions that he had entitled Bricks in the Wall, was chosen as the basis for another album.

There's nothing like a financial crisis to focus minds, and as the year unfolded so did the realisation that Pink Floyds's finances were unravelling. Their financial advisors had managed to lose them some £3.3 million before going bankrupt. Not a happy situation in a country where high earners could be taxed as much as 83%. Legal proceedings for fraud and negligence were the result of that business relationship. In tandem with an unusual urgency in the creation of the new album.

As the year progressed and the true impact of the impending financial Armageddon hanging over them became drastically apparent — bankruptcy, in other words — the band would follow advice to leave the United Kingdom as soon as possible and not return for a full year. Only by avoiding tax as non residents could they avoid financial wipeout.

Early on, the decision was taken that the new album would have to be a double album. That was going to be an enormous challenge, so an outside producer was engaged,

RIGHT: Roger Waters performing a hotel room scene as part of 'The Wall' tour, 1980

and he had to be on the same wavelength as Waters to avoid catastrophe. Canadian producer and keyboardist Robert Allen "Bob" Ezrin was brought in to oversee the project. Ezrin was responsible for the fullness of sound that the album achieved; that sound was due in part to his copying the 16-track drum and bass recordings onto a 24 track for syncing later. The producer's secondary and absolutely vital role was to act as intermediary between the two leading ideas men in Pink Floyd and try to head off a train crash.

Excited by what he heard in the demos, and far from demotivated by the amount of work required to bring it up to scratch, Ezrin took on the job, and in one mammoth nocturnal session beat out a script; forty-eight pages following the life of a character who would later be christened Pink. It was based on Roger Waters' own life, the loss of his father, a domineering mother and despotic schoolteachers, although Ezrin, sensing that it needed a broader thematic palette, was instrumental in making the lead character an amalgamation of all dissatisfied rockers, a rebel for all tastes. Pink's disillusionment and increasing isolation mirrored Water's own, however, as his band mates wryly noted, initially thinking that this was Waters once again panning his litany of life complaints for material in the Roger Waters' psychotherapy hour.

Waters knew that he was in a unique position of control that might never come again, and he had planned that the project would spawn a movie and a stage show. Gerald Scarfe was engaged for the animation, both artists feeding from the creative input of the other. The enormity of the task seemed to make Waters even more megalomaniacal than before, and he was told by Ezrin in no uncertain terms to back off, much to the joy of the 'muffins', as Waters derisively dubbed the other band members. Ezrin's was no easy task, trying to act as go-between and keep everyone motivated whilst draining off some of the artistic monopoly that Waters had assumed for himself.

With the taxman bearing down on them, the decision was made to continue the project at the Super Bear Studios close to Nice in the south of France. Thus the band decamped for their year of exile abroad.

The French flair did nothing to smooth over the increasingly barbed relationship between Waters and Ezrin, who was left feeling vulnerable beneath Water's undiminished, passive-aggressive onslaughts. Ezrin was also going through marital problems and therefore under a personal emotional onslaught as well. Added to this, the musicians' wives had brought their own evil intent along with them from England.

There was also the thorny question of Rick Wright wanting to have a producer role and sitting in on every session, which irked Bob Ezrin and only stopped once Wright had been made aware that his presence was not really wanted.

Nonetheless, apparently helped along with social cocaine use, the band worked to a very strict schedule of 10 to 6; not the usual Floyd method, but thoughts of the British taxman kept their noses to the grindstone. Fortunately, they hardly ever needed to be in the studio together, especially as Mason's drum tracks were finished first and Wright preferred to turn up at night to work when everyone else had gone. Wright needed the less pressured atmosphere to be creative, something understood by Bob Ezrin, not, perhaps, by Roger Waters. Ezrin was not always present in France; he had to oversee recording sessions in New York, where the New York Philharmonic and the New York Symphony Orchestra had been engaged together with a New York City Opera choir.

The pressure increased when Columbia offered a better deal if they could finish the album before the Christmas season kicked in, which meant hiring a second studio and Ezrin whizzing between Waters in one and Gilmour in the other. The two musicians *"...had some pretty major arguments"* at the time according to David Gilmour. Nonetheless, Gilmour knew that their musical relationship was producing some superb work and that it needed to be protected at all costs. And the fraught, competitive nature of their relationship often resulted in the birth of superb songs, such as 'Nobody Home', written after Waters had gone home in a sulk.

MAIN IMAGE: Stage set for 'The Wall' concert on 27th February 1980 at Nassau Coliseum in Long Island, NY

68

Wright's marital problems had worsened, with divorce and animosity between him and his first wife; he would later describe himself during this period of his life as being depressed. But what Gilmour and Waters were acutely aware of was Wright's non-participation, and it was beginning to irritate his bandmates. When Waters worked out a schedule that would cut into the prearranged August holidays, Wright, holidaying with his young children on the Greek island of Rhodes, refused to come earlier, saying he would arrive on the agreed date.

What happened next takes on a different colouring depending on who is telling the story. But it's certain that when Wright arrived in Los Angeles to continue recording, he was told that Waters wanted him to leave the band. Gilmour was less dogmatic, although he did make clear to the keyboard player that he, too, was dissatisfied with Wright's failure to engage. There was even a suggestion that Gilmour had wanted Mason to be given the order of the boot as well.

Waters' threat was that Pink Floyd would not be allowed to release the album if Wright stayed; Waters considered that it was his project alone.

After days of soul-searching, Wright decided to finish the album, do the live shows, and leave the band. The music press wasn't told. Wright's reserved character had been anathema to Waters' aggressive nature ever since their days at Regent Street Polytechnic. The boil had finally burst.

In order to keep the peace moving along, session musicians were brought in, not something Floyd normally wanted to do, and Bob Ezrin got down to editing the tape loops and recording the myriad sound effects without which no Floyd album was complete; the smashing of crockery and a TV set, and screeching tyres to name but three.

Bob Ezrin had taken the initiative in introducing a disco beat to one of the songs. Having done so, Ezrin then saw the potential in what would become 'Another Brick in the Wall (Part 2)', as a single, but at the point that Ezrin realised that it was hit material, Waters was savagely unconvinced. Unfazed,

Ezrin put a track together that included a choir of school children. He then replayed the track to Waters, who suddenly became aware of what he had almost stymied; a world-class hit song. When it was released on the 16th of November 1979, Floyd's single went to number one in the US, the UK, France, Germany, South Africa, and a host of other countries. Everyone was astonished. Needless to say, the conservative contingent of the press was up in arms.

But the internal arguments continued unabated. The arguments over the track 'Comfortably Numb' had been particularly inflammatory. No one disputed the superb construction, but Ezrin and the band divided into camps over a soft or hard version. It eventually acquired an orchestra, with Gilmour's biting guitar solo finally leading it out. The discussions became so rancorous that the song proved to be, as Gilmour said, *"… the last embers of mine and Roger's ability to work collaboratively together"*.

Columbia Records was horrified by what they heard coming through the loudspeakers; discordant, in places militaristic, in places disco sound, mammoth sound effects, a cracking heavy-metal contribution in 'In the Flesh', and comparisons with Kurt Weil's hard-hitting A Beggar's Opera rather than Dark Side of the Moon. Which was the style Columbia would have preferred.

The Wall was released into the streets to begin building its subversive reputation on the 30th of November 1979, by which time the single, 'Another Brick in the Wall (Part 2)' had already rocketed to success with a tail of relief falling away behind it.

The reaction in the music press can best be described as perplexed viciousness. *"Self-centred pessimism"* from the NME, *"Utterly compelling"* from Melody Maker, *"… unremittingly dismal and acidulous"* but *"a stunning synthesis of Waters' by now familiar thematic obsessions"* from Rolling Stone. For The Village Voice it was *"too-kitschy minimal maximalism with sound effects and speech fragments"*. Enclosed in its cover, ironically the quietest that Floyd had yet conceived — a white brick

70

wall — it topped the Billboard charts for 15 weeks, sold 1 million copies in two months, and is now one of the best-selling albums of all time in the US. For his hard work, sound engineer James Guthrie garnered a Grammy award for Best Engineered Recording (non-classical) in 1980.

Incidentally, that album cover was the first that Thorgerson had not designed, due to an argument that led Waters and Thorgerson to estrangement for 25 years; Thorgerson had included the sleeve for Animals in a book he had written; to Waters' great displeasure — displeasure which was leading the Floyd singer and bassist to distancing himself from a great many people. He struck Bob Ezrin off his visiting list when the producer explained what the show was about to a friend of his who couldn't get to see a gig. The *"friend"* then repaid Ezrin by blowing the information to the press. And Waters' ideas were increasingly seen as hypocritical arrogance; his desire to build a permanent wall between the band and the audience (an idea torpedoed by Gilmour) or having an inflatable pig defecate on the audience — those without whom he would be whistling lonely into the wind. His contempt for the hand that fed him also led him to mock his audience during six nights at Earls Court in London. Neither could he keep the lid on his and the band's disagreements amongst themselves, which, he confessed in an interview, had been bubbling for seven years.

It's an interesting side note that, without exception, anyone coming into professional contact with Gilmour and Waters for the first time were nonplussed, initially unable to reconcile Pink Floyd's public image with the very English attitudes and lifestyles of its two leading members offstage.

The band had their reservations about the album; Gilmour, once again, didn't see eye to eye with Waters' cynical opinions, whilst Wright, now in the schizophrenic position of being in the band but not of it, professed not to be happy with all of the music. Waters, on the other hand, thought that it was *"stupefyingly good"*. It was, as Mark Blake wrote, *"grown up rock music with a message"*. Pink Floyd had plucked their era's chord of discontent, and it resonated into the very souls of young people and stirred the fears of those in authority over them.

The band, wearing a Wall uniform of black shirts with an embroidered hammer insignia (occasionally abandoned when Waters sported a white T-shirt with a large number one on it — no megalomania there, then) toured in support of the new album throughout 1980 and 1981, although there were only 31 concerts, modest in comparison to most Floyd tours. Gerald Scarfe was once again responsible for animations that would play on a circular screen above the stage and the wall. It was a huge undertaking. No chance of a drink before the show, as Gilmour explained, because with *"great piles of cue sheets hanging over my amps"* the chances of complete disaster were too great.

71

And when the wall finally crashed to stupendous sound (and a tour loss of $600,000) the audience — despite the fact that The Wall was *"extremely dour"*, as Roger Waters confessed later — knew they had seen something special — as did the promoter Larry Magid, who offered them $2 million for two nights in Philadelphia. Which Waters turned down, refusing to play another stadium.

Away from Floyd, Ginger had now given David a second child, Clare, to pad around in the former 14th century Tudor monastery in Oxfordshire that was soon to be theirs.

Roger Waters was already involved in plans for a film of The Wall, whilst Nick Mason was completing his first solo album, with songs by Carla Bley, a jazz vocalist. It was entitled 'Nick Mason's Fictitious Sports', but it failed to chart.

However, it was the film that was now beginning to take over Waters' thoughts.

The band played a series of gigs in Germany, which the director Alan Parker watched in astonished admiration. After it proved impossible to film the live act, Parker came up with the idea of animated sequences and actors, but no dialogue, moving the story forward with 'The Wall' music providing the soundtrack. When it was certain that Waters was incapable of holding down the lead role, Bob Geldof from the Boomtown Rats, contemptuous of both Pink Floyd and the album, was persuaded to be in the film by a large quantity of dollar signs

With Bob Hoskins and Joanne Whalley now also on-board, Parker began the shooting schedule, which was restricted to 60 days. Wise and observant man that he was, Parker had managed to get Waters to take a break for six weeks, whilst Gerald Scarfe had 50 artists wearing their fingers down to produce almost 15,000 hand-coloured drawings.

Fortunately, Parker had the upper hand after Waters returned and the director found himself on the wrong side of Scarfe and Waters' ire. Without him, the investment would look extremely vulnerable, so when he threatened to walk out, the others had to go cap in hand to ask him to return.

73

Unhappy at losing control over what he saw as the story of his own life, Waters turned to re-recording some of the songs — Bob Geldof taking over vocals for 'In the Flesh' for example.

Not surprisingly, Waters did not like the finished movie, disliking the fact that *"... every minute was trying to be full of action"*. Gilmour was in agreement with his colleague for once, feeling that it was unsuccessful.

And in one way it was, according to writer Mark Blake; *"... at times, it's hard to care or sympathise with... Pink, with his self-pity, his pretensions, his narcissism"*.

AS, INDEED, SOME PEOPLE WERE FINDING IT HARD TO COPE WITH ROGER WATERS FOR THE VERY SAME REASONS.

MAIN IMAGE: Projected animation - The Wall Concert

A BOWLFUL OF BELLIGERENTS

G reat Britain, 1982 will be infamous for one extraordinary event; the Falklands War. Impossible for a Roger Waters, whose father had been in the British Army, to ignore an event of such extraordinary consequence. He loathed the jingoistic nationalism whipped up deliberately by Margaret Thatcher's government, feeling that, although war was, on occasion, necessary, this one definitely was not.

He had been intending to put together more material for an album to be called Spare Bricks. The Falklands War changed all that. Eventually renamed The Final Cut, it spawned more arguments between Roger Waters and David Gilmour. Issue one was the extreme political nature of the material, Gilmour never having seen eye to eye with Waters' left-leaning opinions. Gilmour also felt that the album should be made up of new material, not leftovers from The Wall, which the guitarist thought were not up to scratch. Whilst admitting that he could be lazy at times, Gilmour wanted more time to write songs for the album, time which Waters did not feel he had. Nor did he feel that Gilmour would come up with the goods in any case.

Without soothing words from Ezrin, still banished and in Waters' doghouse, daggers had now been permanently drawn between the two guitarists, as was very evident when the album finally came out in that year of 1982. Gilmour was

vocal lead on just one song. Wright, of course, was already history, replaced and supplemented by a host of session musicians, their presence an extraordinary break with tradition by a band so notoriously insular.

The longer the recording sessions lasted, the more remote the two guitarists became from one another, and the more snow fell onto their relationship. And yet to anyone who didn't know about the undertow, the band members seemed, indeed were, never less than polite to one another. But Gilmour was seething with anger, often driving home in his car screaming to himself in fury after another day when Waters had rejected both his ideas and his music. His name disappeared from the producer credits.

Waters, too, was reaching the limits of his endurance. Even Mason, who had, until then, been someone that Waters could rely on to side with him, deserted him and took up Gilmour's cause. The sessions for Final Cut had not been long underway before Waters knew absolutely that he would never make another album with Mason and Gilmour. He wrested almost total control of the album from their frustrated grasps.

What he produced on an album for which he took all the composing and writing credits, was an album dominated by his, sometimes ranting, aggression-filled singing, marbled with the *"mad tension"* that was the result of them fighting

74

like cats and dogs during sessions that were a misery, in his words. He was slated for his pains. Melody Maker trashed it, calling it *"a milestone in the history of awfulness"*, and in NME, Richard Cook opined that *"Roger Waters' writing has been blown to hell ... The Final Cut isolates and juggles the identical themes of that elephantine concept with no fresh momentum to drive them. "...has the weight of years of self-pity behind it"*, said another critic, although Rolling Stone's Kurt Loder thought that it was *"... a superlative achievement on several levels"*. His *"bleak visions"* did not ride particularly well with the paying customers either, although by May 1983 it had sold over 1 million units. Gilmour felt himself vindicated in his assessment that the material was weak, and he became increasingly dismissive as the years passed. Nonetheless, it did scramble up to number one in the UK and number six in the US, probably thanks to its predecessor, The Wall.

Waters — even his belligerent comments belied the fact that he knew the album was below par — finished off what was essentially his solo project by designing the sleeve — black with a stripe of World War II service medals. It was the last Pink Floyd studio album he would ever work on.

To the outside press world, Waters threw out the gentlemanly line about *"arguments"* and wanting to make a solo album, not mentioning the almost complete breakdown that had taken place.

And where was Barrett when his erstwhile band was in the process of fracturing? He seemed to be deteriorating as quickly as the band and was now living with his mother back in Cambridge in St. Margaret's Square, suffering from stomach ulcers through his poor diet, penniless, fat, and barely able to speak. In the early 80s he spent time in Fulbourn psychiatric hospital, apparently financially supported by his former bandmates. It was a slow demise.

Rick Wright decided he would like to branch out and formed the group Zee with singer and songwriter Dave Harris, front man for the band, Fashion. They recorded in the studio Wright had built, and over the next 18 months they put

the album together. Harris spent a great deal of his time doing his own thing whilst Wright sorted out the emotional aftermath from divorce, coping with the continued presence of his ex-wife and also the gap left in his life after his departure from Floyd.

The album, Identity, was released on the 9th of April 1984, but its new wave, electronic sound — Wright later regretted releasing the album, seeing it as an *"experimental mistake"* — failed to heave itself out of the obscurity of its origins. Fans loved Wright's musicianship but wanted Wright the Floyd man not Wright the Zee man. Wright, though, was floundering emotionally, and no doubt the album, together with his new girlfriend, singer and model Franka, later to become his wife, helped him through a very difficult time.

David Gilmour, went back to his home studio to write songs and be with his family, which had expanded with the arrival of daughter Sara. He then went into the studio to record a second album, About Face, for which he engaged the talents of one Bob Ezrin. And a certain songwriter known as Pete Townsend. It was released in 1984 to reasonably favourable reviews. A *"... well-honed rock album that is riveting from beginning to end"*, wrote the AllMusic critic. It rose to number 21 in the UK and 32 in the US. Gilmour could take satisfaction from the result, knowing that, *"our (Floyd) individual names mean virtually nothing in terms of the great record and ticket-buying public"*. The release was followed by a tour in Europe and North America, and three nights when he was joined by Mason and Wright proved that there were no ill feelings amongst those three members of Floyd, at least.

Waters, the odd man out, was soon off on an American tour of his own with his first solo album, The Pros and Cons of Hitch Hiking. Waters had gone back to retrieve material that had been discarded in favour of The Wall demos. It was a concept album based on the idea of a man dreaming and waking throughout one night and musing on committing adultery with a hitch-hiker picked up on a Californian road trip. Once again, Waters was taking a trip into his own subconscious to see what made an Englishman tick, this

76

time in the realms of sexual encounter; and once again, he produced a happy ending. Something which he rarely enjoyed in reality with Floyd. Later, Waters revealed that the album delved into *"how I felt about my failed marriage, my feelings about sex and all kinds of different areas"*.

What Waters doubtless did enjoy though, was playing alongside Eric Clapton, who he managed to persuade to play on the album. Waters must also have gained great satisfaction from using such a top class guitarist to replace Gilmour.

Gerald Scarfe was once more the creator of graphics and animation for the album, whose controversial cover boasted a rear-view photograph of soft pornography actress Linzi Drew. Naked. Daring for the time.

Released on the 13th of April 1984, Waters' solo album reached 13 in the UK and 31 in the US. In most critics eyes it suffered from being unbalanced; too many words not enough melodies. The *"faintly hideous"* dig from one critic rather says it all.

Nonetheless, with Eric Clapton confirming, to everyone's astonishment, that he was going on tour with Waters, the tour opened in Stockholm on the 16th of June. There were huge screens with animations by Scarfe that mimicked the neuroses being expressed in the lyrics and projected films; the films costing around $400,000. Waters still wanted total control of everything around him, and the strain showed on his face, in his body and in his relationships to those around him, unable to allow others to enjoy themselves when he patently was not. He was also made to realise that Clapton was a bigger star then he was, as audiences hooted when Clapton played solos; a fact reinforced when many concerts had to be cancelled due to lack of interest. Waters' frustration manifested itself one night when he threw his bass down onto the stage and walked off. If he had intended his songs as psychotherapy, they obviously weren't helping him to move forward personally. It was fairly obvious that Clapton no longer wanted to be part of this egotistical eruption that was the world of Roger Waters. Clapton stuck it out until the end, by which time the tour had deflated Waters' finances by some

£400,000. But he wanted to tour, and, unable to let his baby go, he continued to do so in 1985.

Nick Mason also ventured back into the studio to embark on his second album to be called Profiles. David Gilmour, his ambition for a solo career having subsided, sang alongside 10cc guitarist Rick Fenn in what was an entirely instrumental album, except the two songs: 'Lie for a Lie' and 'Israel'. Fenn and Mason would go on to form Bamboo Music, a film and TV commercial music company.

The album was notable for the song 'Lie for a Lie', which was written by Danny Peyronel, the UFO keyboard player and was not only an excellent pop song, but was the first time that Mason and Gilmour came together in what would very shortly be the new Pink Floyd.

Waters had no more interest in the band Pink Floyd, feeling that it was a spent life force. His relationship with the band's manager Steve O'Rourke had never been easy, but he needed Mason and Gilmour to agree to dismiss him. This they refused to do. They were aware of Waters' intentions towards the band, he was publicly proclaiming that Pink Floyd was finished; but unlike him they wished to continue with it. So Waters took matters into his own hands. He went to the High Court to stop the name Pink Floyd being used ever again. Gilmour refused to back down despite Waters' resentful threats to be negative should Gilmour ever attempt to make a record, which Waters felt was never going to happen anyway.

Having engaged former Stones' manager Peter Rudge to manage his affairs, Waters wrote to EMI and Columbia stating that he had left the band. Accusations filled all the channels of communication in the twelve months until the dispute about the name Pink Floyd came to trial.

Waters filled the time with When the Wind Blows, an animated movie for which he created the soundtrack. The resulting album produced less of a hurricane, more of a burp amongst the buying public.

Bob Ezrin suddenly found himself back on the wanted list, phoned, first of all, by Waters, insisting that he was a changed man and wanting to work with the producer, and then by David Gilmour, who wanted Ezrin to listen to some songs he'd made. Which rather surprised Ezrin as he'd been told by Waters that the other members of the band wouldn't dare to carry on without the bass player. But by the time of Gilmour's call, Ezrin's wife had emotionally broken down at the thought of moving lock, stock and barrel to the UK, so the producer called Waters to say he wasn't coming after all. Which sent Waters ballistic. Not so much of a changed man then.

Jabbed into action by Waters' sarcasm, Gilmour was out to win the challenge and spent the summer working with a cast of new musicians. That emotionally electrified summer was given more poignancy by a phone call to Gilmour from Rick Wright's wife Franka asking if the keyboard player could participate in the new album. Gilmour was happy to oblige, knowing that three former members was better than two in the eyes of the public, although there was a clause in Wright's leaving agreement preventing him from rejoining as a full member of Floyd. Gilmour knew that Wright would also strengthen the band musically.

Gilmour and Ezrin agreed to work together partly in England and partly in Los Angeles, the guitarist being much more accommodating than Waters. As they settled into work in an idyllic setting on the Astoria, Gilmour's houseboat studio close to Hampton Court, the repercussions from the personal acrimony started to resolve into their ugly shapes. Lawyers' calls constantly interrupted the sessions. O'Rourke began proceedings against Waters for £25,000 of unpaid commissions, whilst in October, Waters began his own proceedings to dissolve the Pink Floyd partnership; and continued being derogatory about his former bandmates' musical abilities. Even Gilmour, however, confessed that without Waters' driving force, the creative process was much more difficult. But nothing short of death would have stopped Gilmour. There must have been times when Gilmour thought it would come to that, especially as Waters was still a shareholder and director of Pink Floyd music and therefore had the right to veto any decisions. A right that he exercised in full, of course, when he came down to the Astoria for meetings.

A side issue was Mason's inability to play. His confidence seemed to have vanished, which meant that computer technology had to step in to relieve the immediate need. And there was also an immediate need for a songwriter, one that was filled by singer-songwriter Anthony Moore. He was co-writer on the song 'Learning to Fly', which proved a pivotal work for everyone concerned, proving, firstly, that they could produce a good song and secondly, that they could produce a good song that sounded like Pink Floyd. They knew that they had learned how to fly. But Gilmour wanted to fly quickly, because Waters was also in the process of making an album.

Revamped, Pink Floyd decamped to Los Angeles to work with Ezrin there. Then they needed to put the material to the test on the road.

At which point, Waters sent letters to all the North American promoters threatening to sue them if they sold Pink Floyd tickets. Neither was there any advance money from the record company to fund the tour, so Mason and Gilmour had to dig into their own pockets. But the promoters ignored the threat, with three shows alone promising a $3 million income. Pink Floyd, it seemed, were back in business.

If Waters didn't manage to jump on them in court first.

With Thorgerson back on board for the album cover — 700 empty beds on a Devon beach — Floyd christened their baby A Momentary Lapse of Reason. Which gave rise to the predicted and predictable darts from Waters, who brought out his second album, Radio K.A.O.S., on June the 15th 1985. Waters' lyrical and conceptual ability and his commitment to an idea were never in doubt. But the density of his layered cake and his attempts at modernity proved his undoing. And he topped his previous grim themes with an exploration of the mind of a mentally and physically disabled man. It climbed up to 25 in the UK and 50 in the United States, but the reviews were mixed and the tour failed to ignite; a dissatisfied Waters confessed later, *"I should never have made that record"*.

Now it was Pink Floyd's turn to show what they could do without Waters.

Summer was over it was the 7th of September 1987. Gilmour's album was a departure from the format of previous albums in that it was not a concept album but a collection of songs. It fired up the charts after its release and despite Waters' derision there was nothing he could do to stop it from heading to number three in both the UK and the US. So Gilmour could feel well pleased by *"A chillingly beautiful vocal exploration"* as the track 'A New Machine' was described. He was now undeniably Mr. Pink Floyd, even though it was hardly likely to challenge Waters in terms of its lyrics. But Gilmour had put his stamp on it, he had finally been able to *"... focus more on the music, restore the balance"*.

"Learning to Fly", written by David Gilmour, Anthony Moore, Bob Ezrin and Joe Carin, was uncoupled from the album and released as a single on the 14th of September. It moved up to number one on the Billboard Album Rock Track chart.

The rehearsals for the tour, with Guy Pratt replacing Roger Waters, turned out to be chaotic, as no one could remember how to play anything. Bob Ezrin was brought in to sort out problems, which he duly did *"Until the baby was walking"*. There was a lot to sort out; it was a Floyd show, after all, so there was an 80-foot high, steel framework, dry ice and a circular screen. Plus the flying pig, a giant mirror ball and an aeroplane. These would wrap around a first-half dedicated to the new album and a second-half to some of Floyd's great oldies, which were given additional zest by the younger band members athletically moving around the stage, and the fizzing special effects.

80

MAIN IMAGE: Pink Floyd performing on the A Momentary Lapse of Reason Tour, 1987

Waters' and Gilmour's shows were touring at the same time, just to add an even sharper competitive edge to their antagonisms.

Waters was firing brickbats at the band whenever possible; $35,000 in copyright fees for the use of his flying pig, which Floyd circumvented by placing large genitals beneath it.

The attrition couldn't go on much longer, the conflict had to come to a head. Lawyers for Waters discovered that the Pink Floyd partnership had never been confirmed, so Waters attempted to stop his former band members from using the name. But Waters sensed that he was on a hiding to nothing. Many years later he said that he had been threatened that he would be responsible for loss of earnings and legal expenses and would suffer withdrawal of royalties if he prevented the band from making any more records, because of the product commitment with CBS. *"They forced me to resign from the band, because if I hadn't, the financial repercussions would have wiped me out completely"*. So Waters agreed to settle the dispute.

It was over. A vile and destructive period for everyone had come to an end. On the 23rd of December 1987, an agreement was signed which allowed Gilmour and Mason to use the name Pink Floyd in perpetuity. Waters would keep control of various aspects of the band's activities; the most important of these was The Wall.

"I was wrong, of course I was", said Waters in 2013, referring to his lawsuit.

IT WAS A VERY SAD ENDING FOR EVERYONE.

81

BACK ON THE
MAGIC ROUNDABOUT

At least the antagonisms were now catapulted from a distance and not from close quarters in the boardroom. Nonetheless, Waters resentment could leave no snippet of information about the reformed Floyd unmolested, although Gilmour and Mason could be fairly relaxed about it when they looked at the glowing sales figures for the new album and glanced into the full stadiums as they toured the world.

And the Phoenix Floyd members spread a distinctly more amiable atmosphere around them; there was none of the intense introspection and intellectual agonising that had aggravated and isolated them from one another in the past. The lads were very happy to cram into the band van with everyone else and the alcohol — followed, to everyone's amusement, by their empty limousines. Everyone felt it, what was described as *"tremendous spirit"* and a sense of liberation. A party mood broke out with all that that entailed in a rock star's life; including meditation and cocaine.

With Gilmour's wife, Ginger, slowly fading into the distance, he felt it was time to indulge himself, and he led his bachelor life from a townhouse in Little Venice in London accompanied by kaleidoscopic companions. Later in life, he wished he hadn't taken cocaine, but he recognised that the intense legal wranglings, his marital problems, the financial cliff-edge on which they had perched and the years-long tensions within the band had worn him down. Dangerously, he had become a

party animal. Anyone could fall off the twig as Syd Barrett had done; Syd, who was still alive but frequented mental hospitals and about whom rumour said that he daubed himself in white powder and spoke gibberish.

In between partying, the lads went back out on tour in the UK and Europe sparked into renewed vigour by the fresh blood and enthusiasm of the new band members, bass player Guy Pratt, keyboard player Jon Carin and drummer Gary Wallis, and wanting to conquer the world. Wright and Gilmour were the custodians of the Floyd flame, as Guy Pratt found out, and the guitarist was enthused to find that the Floyd sound was produced from a synthesis of the two long-time Floyd musicians working closely together.

They kept the product flowing with Delicate Sound of Thunder, a live album that contained the last five nights of the tour, in New York. It threaded its way up to number 11 in both the UK and the US and also went up into space with Russian astronauts in the Soyuz TM 7 rocket.

For nearly 18 months, the band became wandering minstrels around Europe, until they finally pulled down the pig in Marseille on the 18th of July 1989. They had grossed $135 million and had proven that even without Roger Waters they could raise the bar higher still, and the extravagant scale of their shows became the benchmark for live performances.

RIGHT: Pink Floyd's inflatable pig above the stage at Wembley Arena, London, 1988

83

MAIN IMAGE: First date of Another Lapse tour, Belgium 1989

BACK ON THE MAGIC ROUNDABOUT

Back in England, the new decade of the 1990s began with an appearance at the open-air venue of Knebworth Park, where Pink Floyd performed in curtains of rain whipped by high winds in the company of Phil Collins, Eric Clapton, Jimmy Page and Cliff Richard. It was a suitably dramatic situation that was the herald of the band's three-year absence from performing in public.

Roger Waters, on the other hand, had no intention of either hiding himself from the public eye or restraining himself from tossing barbs at his former bandmates, and in July 1990, he decided to perform The Wall close to the Brandenburg Gate in Berlin as a post fall-of-the-wall celebration. Despite a glittering cast, the resulting album only just managed to drag itself into the UK top 30 but failed to get into the US top 50. Which was probably gratifying to the Pink Floyd musicians, who had not been invited. Although, apparently, their wives had been.

It was quite a year for Waters who, once he had left EMI, concluded a new worldwide deal with Columbia, his label in United States. He also found himself a new manager, Mark Fenwick, and after 16 years, he left his wife for Priscilla Phillips, an American actress.

What were the Floyd men up to if they weren't playing in public. Well, Nick Mason divorced and married Annette Linton a TV presenter and actress, and David Gilmour also got divorced and almost killed himself when he took part in the Carrera Pan American sports car race with Steve O'Rourke and drove over an embankment. The event had been filmed, so Floyd set to work to write music for the soundtrack, bringing back the musicians who had worked with them on the Momentary Lapse Tour. They enjoyed themselves immensely whilst jamming for what turned out to be a less than successful effort produced in double quick time. Following that, Gilmour seemed content to enjoy life without pressure as a session musician on other people's albums.

Waters finally divorced Carolyne Christie in 1992, the year he released his third studio album, Amused to Death, the conclusion of many years of work, a five-year recording period, which ended a five-year hiatus between albums since radio K.A.O.S. In it, Waters' themes once again ranged over a variety of world-scarring events such as the first Gulf War and Tiananmen Square and explored TVs influence. Mostly negative, he decided.

Waters had gone for quality musicians, with stars of the calibre of Don Henley, guitar maestro Jeff Beck, and Rita Coolidge joining him in the studio. Sadly, even then Waters' resentment at perceived wrongs — Bob Ezrin was the target in this case — found its way into the lyrics.

Whatever his loud protests about the men in grey suits, Waters decided he needed them to promote his album, which hit the streets on the 1st of September 1992. The singer could be well pleased with his finished work. And, indeed, he was, considering it an *"absolutely classic"* album. For the first time, one of his albums reached the UK top 10 settling on number eight. It also reached number 21 on the Billboard 200, another first. It did get some good reviews — amongst those that said that it was *"nowhere near"* The Wall or Dark Side of the Moon. Waters without Floyd was, it seems, overflow lyrics, underflow musical lyricism.

Mason and Gilmour popped up at some charity concerts in 1992, and by the following year, the year that Roger Waters married Priscilla, everyone in Pink Floyd returned refreshed to the studio with the difficult years now behind them. Gilmour was also enjoying the blossoms of a new love with the newspaper journalist Polly Samson. And Polly turned out to be more than just a pretty face. She moved from supporting Gilmour in his musical adventures to becoming a songwriter, and although her increasing presence in the studio caused tensions in the boy's club of the management, Ezrin, for one, was wise enough to realise the powerful inspirational effect Polly Samson was having on her boyfriend. Wisely, because a pivotal song turned out to be one entitled 'High Hopes', which Gilmour and Samson wrote in tandem and one that drew together the threads of the album, with its rounded emotions and clarity, as Ezrin freely admitted. It became the musical highlight of the album.

At that point, Wright was still not a full member of the band, something that irked him so intensely — feeling that he was being unfairly treated — that he almost refused to make the planned album. But he did end up with five co-writing credits. And with Gilmour, Mason and Wright jamming, more or less, carefree in the studio, they compiled well over 60 pieces of music, which they eventually slimmed down to eleven songs. It hadn't been intended as a concept album, but there was a theme; the importance of communication in preventing interpersonal breakdown.

With Guy Pratt, Gary Wallis and John Carin back on board, work proceeded apace, and after a break in September for a one-off live performance for charity, December rolled around and the project neared completion. They had found a title, too; or rather, a friend, the author of 'The Hitchhiker's Guide to the Galaxy', Douglas Adams, came up with one; Division Bell. And Storm Thorgerson came up with the striking cover image of two monolithic Easter Island-like heads facing each other and thus forming a third head, *"the absent face"*, as Thorgerson commented, invoking the missing Syd Barrett. Barrett, indeed, was on Gilmour's mind once again in the first verse of 'Poles Apart'; or was it Roger Waters — who was extremely unhappy with having been supplanted as lyricist by Polly Samson and was now becoming rather a bore in making his views loudly known; and he would certainly have hated what happened next.

The Division Bell was released on the 28th of March 1994. It hit number one in the UK and the US, and despite some less than complimentary reviews it was nominated for "Best Album by a British Artist" for the 1995 Brit awards. Floyd even received a Grammy for the track 'Marooned' for the "Best Rock Instrumental Performance". A *"glib, vacuous cipher of an album"* was just one arrow-headed review. But its themes of unfulfilled hopes, of communication cul-de-sacs, connected well with audiences, the only critics who truly matter. The album had woven a memory of the style of Floyd of yesteryear, stoically sticking to its guns despite new generations of musicians grasping for musical credence around them in any way they could. This confidence in themselves was evident in the band's

music. And David Gilmour, for one, was happy with what he described as the *"lumbering beast"* that was Pink Floyd.

What no one could have realised at the time was that an era was drawing to a close; the lumbering beast would not produce another album for twenty years and when it did pull another one out of the hat, it would be based on instrumental work put together during the making of The Division Bell; and the beast was also about to embark on its very last tour.

An air force space in North Carolina was chosen to be the rehearsal rooms for the planned tour. The challenge was to equal the sparkling show that had been the Momentary Lapse of Reason Tour. So, with an apparently limitless budget, two cargo planes and a Russian freight plane were hired to ferry around the two huge pigs, 300 speakers, a circular 40 foot screen, lasers and the 400 varilights needed to keep 200 crew members busy for the night. Two extra stages ensured that work could begin in advance for the two following venues.

Shortly after the album's release, Pink Floyd opened a tour in Miami with a set that included Astronomy Domine, Momentary Lapse of Reason, The Division Bell and tracks from Wish You Were Here, The Wall and the Dark Side of the Moon. They brought their wives and girlfriends with them — and, on occasion, also the children — as they moved through the US and Canada, which ensured that there would be no rock 'n' roll lifestyles for the older band members on this tour. Which didn't go down very well with the younger musicians. Polly Samson's role was still resented on many sides, meaning that tension was never very far away.

By July, the tour had arrived in Europe, and in that same month, Gilmour married Polly, who, by that time, was earning royalties from her work on the Division Bell. In a gesture of goodwill, the band invited Roger Waters to come and play with them during the final 14 nights at Earls Court in London. Gilmour genuinely felt that this conciliatory meeting would be a wonderful moment for the fans. But he had a little doubt that Waters would refuse. He did. Managing, for once, to forgo the acerbic barbs.

88

PINKFLOYD A Kaleidoscope of Conundrums

MAIN IMAGE: Pink Floyd live in Chantilly, France on 31st July 1994

90

MAIN IMAGE: Toronto Canada 1994

On the 29th of October 1994, the tour came to an end.

Pink Floyd would never tour again.

Over 5 million people had watched the shows and brought in a gross income of some $100 million. If David Gilmour had wanted to prove that he could go it alone without Roger Waters, he had done a magnificent job. He needed now to prove nothing else, and he was tired of the rigours of touring life. Even the live album of the tour, released in June 1995 and given the title Pulse, vindicated him by reaching number one in the UK and the US, not to mention Canada, Germany, Australia and a host of other countries.

Rick Wright, perhaps sensing that Floyd was winding down, was inspired to start work on his second solo album. Work was already well underway by the time The Division Bell Tour ended, and apart from some Floyd regulars, Sinead O'Connor came to the studio to do her turn for him. The result was Broken China, a concept album in four parts in which he explored his ex-wife's struggle with depression. He was aware of the moral dilemma, but perhaps this was a cathartic exercise for the keyboard player, as anyone who has lived with a depressive partner is often left with unresolved guilt. Wright had expressed himself not to be one hundred percent satisfied with musical ambience of The Division Bell, wishing that it had been given a more distinctively Pink Floyd style. He nobly tried to re-capture this in Broken China, but the album failed to ignite the passions of anyone but the most intense Floyd fans.

Before the year was out, Pink Floyd had been inducted into the Rock and Roll Hall of Fame – and David Gilmour turned 50.

And then the Pink Floyd musicians settled into peaceful lives, with David Gilmour trading his vintage aeroplanes and classic cars and reassessing his life in his West Sussex farmhouse. He appeared content to make guest appearances on other musicians' tracks without having to undergo the wear and tear of Pink Floyd. Rick Wright sailed his yacht and looked after his young son.

Roger Waters was the first to break back to the surface, performing a series of live dates in 1999, which he entitled Roger Waters in the Flesh. The shows contained many past Pink Floyd songs, including those from The Wall, but also a new song that Waters had written as his finalé; 'Each Small Candle'. The tour would be a great success and eventually spanned three years and the world. The performances spawned a re-mastered movie of The Wall — and a brief and awkward meeting between Waters and Wright, who had gone backstage, fed up with the continuing feud.

93

AND THAT IS HOW PINK FLOYD ENTERED THE NEW MILLENNIUM.

LOOKING FORWARD TO THE PAST

March of the year 2000 was graced with the album, Is There Anybody out There? The Wall Live: Pink Floyd 1980—81, released to celebrate the 20th anniversary of The Wall. Apart from a bit of sniping, all passed off peacefully.

But a warning of things yet to come occurred the following year, 2001, with the death of Judy Trim, Waters' first wife, and Gilmour found himself performing at a memorial service for his friend the author Douglas Adams. He also put together some songs for a show at the Royal Festival Hall in London and in Paris, and as far as he was concerned, Pink Floyd would not be producing anything in the near future. He was, he said, working on putting together a new solo album; Pink Floyd would be left to languish in musical memory, glowing like a strange jewel.

There was a more encouraging reconciliation in 2002 when a chance encounter between Nick Mason and Roger Waters in the Caribbean led to Mason joining Waters on tour in London in June. Waters was heading towards his 60s and finally metamorphosing into an adult, as he confessed himself. He was passing through the emotional wringer again as another marriage broke down. Nonetheless, he was still able to get very *"grumpy"*, according to Gilmour, when it came to choosing a song list for a new EMI release; Echoes: The Best of Pink Floyd. But Waters was able to choose his own favourites, many of them put together in Flickering Flame: The Solo Years Part 1, which contained what he felt

were his best songs. They came with an acknowledgement of sorts that he had perhaps overindulged his pet dislikes when writing previous songs and that not everyone was interested.

In 2003, came the first of the heavy slaps in the face from mortality when Floyd's manager since 1968, Steve O'Rourke, died from a stroke in Miami. Gilmour found himself alongside Richard Wright and Nick Mason when they played at his funeral service in November. Only a metamorphosing Roger Waters could not bring himself to attend. The band had already lost tour manager Tony Howard, and within weeks their arranger/orchestrator Michael Kamen was dead from a heart attack.

Nick Mason, meanwhile, finished the book that he was working on dealing with his life in Pink Floyd, entitled Inside Out: A Personal History of Pink Floyd. It was accompanied by a book signing tour, and, interestingly, Roger Waters agreed to comment — his comments brought forth the revelation that he and Gilmour were not about to reconcile.

And yet. What a difference a year makes.

Bob Geldof was putting together Live 8 in 2005, and he became obsessed with the idea of a reunited Pink Floyd on stage at London's Hyde Park. Refusing to take Gilmour's no for an answer, he visited and wrote to the guitarist; to no avail — until Gilmour received a telephone call.

RIGHT: Pink Floyd taking a bow at the Live 8 concert in Hyde Park, London 2nd July 2005

It was Roger Waters.

The call only lasted a few minutes, their first conversation in two years, but they discussed the possibility of getting back together, and after thinking about it for twenty-four hours, Gilmour decided that it would be a mistake not to agree. He felt that the *"petty"* personal arguments paled into insignificance when confronted with the problems of Africa that Live 8 was trying to highlight and alleviate. He phoned Waters. With Wright on board as well, four of the original band members would come together.

Pink Floyd would play again.

Not that Waters was quite so relaxed with his decision; but he bravely fought with his instincts, initially believing that he would sing his more aggressive songs from The Wall. Gilmour objected, pointing out that *"we don't need no education" was not, perhaps, the best message to be sending out from a Live 8 stage to Africa. The metamorphosed Waters succumbed to the weight of reason for a higher cause. "For one night only"*.

Waters, who at some point in life had upset everyone gathered to support Pink Floyd's Live 8, proved to be prickly in more than just his song list choices. Gilmour wanted a smaller circle of musicians, a *"compact"* set; not so Waters. This coming together was not amicable, it was *"awkward and uncomfortable"* in Gilmour's words. But the lads at least hid, even if they didn't bury, the hatchet for eighteen glorious minutes of music making that shone brightly and brought tears to many an eye.

The occasion had Waters grinning manically at the end of the set, and the group hug onstage seemed to induce a flare up of magnanimity in the bass player; *"I regret my part in that negativity"* was his comment on twenty years of Floyd at loggerheads. Pink Floyd members had, he added, created a *"very, very, special thing"*. Metamorphosis indeed. Or maybe he had finally realised that what he had thought was true was not; Roger Waters alone was not Pink Floyd.

Neither did he slam the door on the idea of more performances with his erstwhile colleagues. For charity only. Stoked up by Live 8, Waters set off on a resurrected tour of In the Flesh the following year.

Gilmour did not feel like being magnanimous. He turned down huge offers for reunion concerts. There would be no more albums and no more tours, and the Live 8 rehearsals had simply confirmed what he already knew; although pointing no fingers, he did not want to be part of that stressful world again. Wright kept his counsel to himself whilst Mason was packed and ready to go, he said.

Unbeknownst to anybody, time was running out.

So the fateful year of 2006 came around and began with a dose of reality for hopeful Pink Floyd fans.

Interviewed in an Italian newspaper in February, Gilmour said, *"I am 60 years old. Pink Floyd was an important part of my life, I have had a wonderful time, but it's over. For me, it's much less complicated to work alone"*.

One month later, on March the 6th, Gilmour's third solo album, On an Island, was released. Its elegiac and very English ambience evoking nostalgia and even melancholy, with lyrics crafted and co-crafted by Polly Samson, had *"a feeling of contentment to it"* in Gilmour's words. Celebrated Polish film composer Zbigniew Preisner arranged the orchestrations. Gilmour dedicated the album to his lost fellow journeymen along the Pink Floyd road, Michael Kamen and Tony Howard. Inevitably, therefore, undertones of mortality threaded through the tracks. And as though to underline the validity of Gilmour's themes, Floyd engineer Nick Griffiths died that very month.

Gilmour had good reason to be satisfied with his work. The album was number 1 in the UK, number 2, in Canada and number 1 in Europe, also coming in at number six in the US. It was Gilmour's first non-Pink Floyd number 1.

The tour in support of the album began on March the 7th, with Gilmour accompanied by Rick Wright — Gilmour was always appreciative of Wright's beautiful playing — who gave superb performances and was enthusiastically greeted everywhere. Even David Bowie popped up in one of the shows, as did David Crosby and Graham Nash.

And in the middle of good music and enjoyment as they toured through North America and Europe, the news that everyone had feared for so long finally came through.

It was the 7th of July 2006, a Friday. Syd Barrett was 60 years old and died peacefully at home in Cambridge from pancreatic cancer.

Syd had faded from his former friends' lives long before he slipped away permanently. No one but his closest family knew any longer who had lived inside Syd Barrett. The man who bequeathed £1.25 million to his brothers and sisters had lost three fingers from complications due to diabetes, and evolved into a Cambridge eccentric, cycling around town, a romantic fantasy frozen in time in the imaginations of many Floyd fans. The *"eccentricity"* veil concealed much darker problems, of course.

None of the Pink Floyd musicians attended the funeral, but Rick Wright called him *"the guiding light of the early band"*, saying that his legacy continued to inspire the musicians that came after him. He was, as Gilmour described him after his death, *"the madcap genius who made us smile"* and who *"touched more people than he could ever know"*. The brief and special light that had once shone in Pink Floyd had finally been extinguished.

Roger Waters had abandoned the UK to live in New York with his new girlfriend Laurie Durning, whilst he continued to tour, and his three-act opera Ça Ira, having been released in September 2005, was staged in September for the second time. He also embarked on a two-year tour of The Dark Side of the Moon Live that launched into Europe in June.

Gilmour released his own version of *"Arnold Layne"* in December 2006 as a tribute to Syd Barrett. Gilmour continued to deny that any version of Pink Floyd would be resuscitated;

the hurt ran too deeply, Waters' intransigence and ego had caused too much damage and put paid to any hope of reconciliation when confronted with Gilmour's obstinacy.

The Piper at the Gates of Dawn celebrated its 40th anniversary in 2007, and this gave rise to a whole host of tributes to the band, and a Syd Barrett tribute concert was planned for the Barbican Centre in London on May the 10th. Wright signed up to attend, Roger Waters was interested, no one knew if Mason or David Gilmour would turn up.

As the first half of the show drew to a close, the audience stood and cheered; Roger Waters was on stage. He spoke of Syd, who *"lived his life like he walked… bounced, the whole time"*. It was, he mused, because Syd was willing to take risks that the band, and Waters himself, owed Barrett such an enormous debt. Thereupon, Water's underdeveloped sensitivity fainted with exhaustion, and he chose an inappropriate song. He had already forgotten that Pink Floyd had been four musicians not one. A disappointed audience hadn't. They were disappointed, too, when Wright, Mason and Gilmour trooped onto the stage without the bass player. Rumours abounded of refusals and prior appointments, but had they all been willing it would, no doubt have been possible.

The three-and-a-half minutes of 'Arnold Layne' sounded out, then it was over. A chance had slipped through their fingers. It would never return. The year 2008 would see to that.

Richard Wright, the keyboard magician who was never happier than when he was on the road or sailing around the Greek islands, had endured considerable pain at the hands of Pink Floyd. They had been too immature to cope with the different sensitivities in his personality, to the extent that he just withdrew into himself finally becoming the victim of Waters' vindictively inflating ego. Once that had been removed, his confidence and his creativity returned, nurtured by a more sensitive David Gilmour. As so often with those who are unassuming and gentle, his talent had been overlooked, and therefore underappreciated. And yet his contribution to the Pink Floyd sound had been absolutely

97

essential, providing untold magical elements.

On the 15th of September, Rick Wright, one of the *"dysfunctional family"*, succumbed to cancer. He was 65 years old. He bequeathed £24 million to his family.

Too late now for a reunion.

Gilmour did not want to tour with the remnants of Pink Floyd again.

Waters, on the other hand, had to keep busy, and his next project was to take out The Wall on its 30th anniversary in 2010. Before it got underway, the second miracle occurred; Waters and Gilmour came together to perform for the Hoping Foundation charity in Oxfordshire in England in July. But still, there had to be negotiating before the *"miracle"* could happen and Waters would take up Gilmour's invitation to play for 200 paying guests. Gilmour sweetened the offer, saying that he would play a one-off in Waters' The Wall in return. And so it was. A delighted and surprised audience heard Gilmour play during 'Comfortably Numb', listening happily to his guitar solos, and they even got Nick Mason thrown in for good measure for 'Outside the Wall'. Waters was overcome with a Road to Damascus-like conversion to Floyd friendship, assured everyone that he was a changed man, and stood with his hand around Gilmour's shoulders, beaming. No one else was quite so convinced. Then they parted.

Life went on without Pink Floyd.

Except for EMI, who, after losing a legal dispute with the band, signed a new contract with them for the sale of Floyd music online. It was, as Gilmour commented, time to set it free, to stop *"hanging on"* to the material. It was almost a farewell to Pink Floyd.

In 2012, the two remaining Floyd men, Mason and Gilmour, began to gather material that had involved Rick Wright, mostly from The Division Bell days. They wanted to indulge in modern studio technology and hired session musicians to bolster an album that was the lads' contribution to showing *"what a special player he was"*, Gilmour commented; how

he had been at the heart of Pink Floyd.

Another gap opened up in Pink Floyd's history in April of 2013 when Storm Thorgerson died. He had been responsible for many of the iconic Floyd covers that had been so striking they had taken on lives of their own, and he was considered one of the best album designers of his era. It had been a bumpy ride for him, too, but his name would always be indelibly linked with the band.

The almost entirely instrumental Endless River, the fifteenth Floyd studio album, arrived on November the 7th 2014, already the most pre-ordered album of all time on Amazon UK, debuting at number 1 in many countries, a fitting tribute to a sadly underrated and often mistreated musician. *"Wright was the steady, binding majesty in Floyd's explorations"*, wrote one reviewer. It was *"unmistakably Floyd"*. It was also seen as Pink Floyd saying goodbye. Gilmour confirmed this saying, *"It's a shame, but this is the end"*.

Rumours that one of Britain's first psychedelic pop groups would ever reunite were firmly laid to rest once again by David Gilmour in 2015. It would, he reiterated, be wrong to reunite without Rick Wright.

2015 was the year the Gilmour went back on tour for the first time in nine years, and the year when his fourth solo studio album took shape; Rattle that Lock. He previewed it in Carlow, Ireland on June the 6th, and it was released on the 18th of September. Europe and South America heard it first, followed by the US and Canada in 2016. Gilmour brought together a host of friends on Rattle That Lock, including old friend Rado Klose. Graham Nash and David Crosby were back as was John Carin, Guy Pratt, the orchestration was by Zbigniew Preisner, and Polly Samson wrote five of the songs with Gilmour penning two. And David's son Gabriel made his debut on piano in 'In Any Tongue'.

Rattle That Lock is a reflection on the passing of time, the passing of Floyd, the shortening span separating Gilmour from his departed colleagues. He was, as Rolling Stone opined, his most eloquent when his guitar sang with *"silvery treble"* and sounding like *"an expressive master of his craft, one who*

98

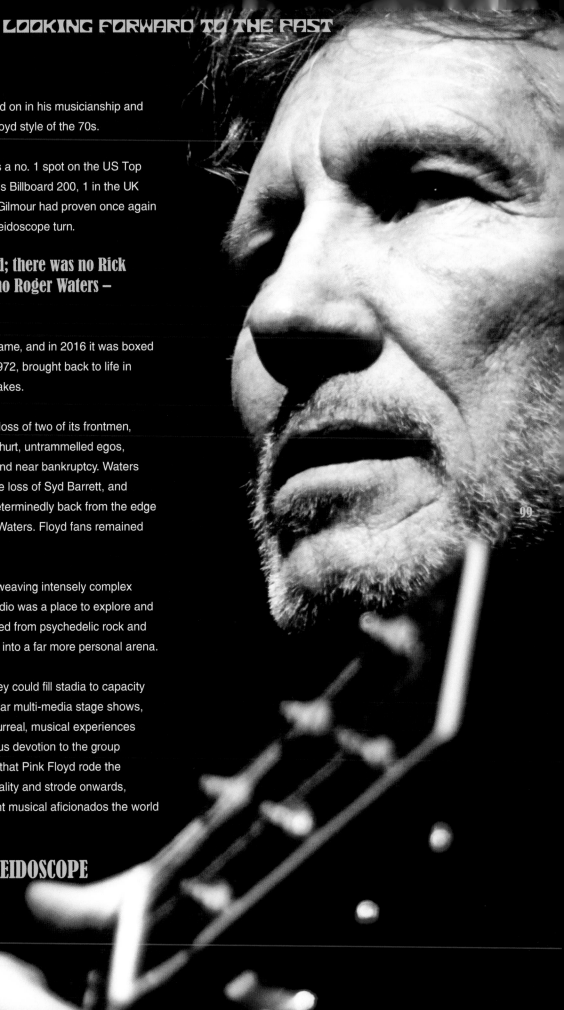

hasn't aged a day". Floyd lived on in his musicianship and his musical nods to the Pink Floyd style of the 70s.

His reward, and Polly's, was a no. 1 spot on the US Top Rock Albums chart, 5 on the Us Billboard 200, 1 in the UK and a host of other countries. Gilmour had proven once again that he could still make the kaleidoscope turn.

But it was not Pink Floyd; there was no Rick Wright, no Nick Mason, no Roger Waters – no Syd Barrett.

Floyd existed now only in name, and in 2016 it was boxed up as The Early Years 1965-1972, brought back to life in films, live recordings, and outtakes.

The band had survived the loss of two of its frontmen, years of internecine strife and hurt, untrammelled egos, struggles for musical identity and near bankruptcy. Waters had taken the band through the loss of Syd Barrett, and David Gilmour had guided it determinedly back from the edge of destruction at the hands of Waters. Floyd fans remained nervously loyal throughout.

Pink Floyd were known for weaving intensely complex musical tapestries, and the studio was a place to explore and expand their ideas, which moved from psychedelic rock and experimental electronic effects into a far more personal arena.

And speaking of arenas, they could fill stadia to capacity with their innovative, spectacular multi-media stage shows, producing some of the most surreal, musical experiences of the era of love. The tenacious devotion to the group by all band members ensured that Pink Floyd rode the tempestuous waves of personality and strode onwards, bruised but unbowed, to delight musical aficionados the world over, as they still do.

PINK FLOYD; A KALEIDOSCOPE OF CONUNDRUMS.

99

PINKFLOYD DISCOGRAPHY

ALBUMS

TITLE	RELEASE DATE	CHART POSITION
The Piper at the Gates of Dawn	4th of August 1967	UK-6 / US-131
A Saucerful of Secrets	28th of June 1968	UK-9
More	13th of June 1969	UK-9 / US-153
Ummagumma	7th of November 1969	UK-5 / US-74
Atom Heart Mother	2nd of October 1970	UK-1 / US-55
Meddle	5th of November 1971	UK-3 / US-70
Obscured by Clouds	2nd of June 1972	UK-6 / US-46
The Dark Side of the Moon	16th of March 1973	UK-2 / US-1
Wish You Were Here	12th of September 1975	UK-1 / US-1
Animals	21st of January 1977	UK-2 / US-3
The Wall	30th of November 1979	UK-3 / US-1
The Final Cut	21st of March 1983	UK-1 / US-6
A Momentary Lapse of Reason	7th of September 1987	UK-3 / US-3
The Division Bell	28th of March 1994	UK-1 / US-1
The Endless River	10th of November 2014	UK-1 / US-3

LIVE ALBUMS

TITLE	RELEASE DATE	CHART POSITION
Delicate Sound of Thunder	21st of November 1988	UK-11 / US-1
Pulse	5th of June 1995	UK-1 / US-1
Is There Anybody out There? The Wall Live 1980-81	27th of March 2000	UK-15 / US-19

COMPILATION ALBUMS

TITLE	RELEASE DATE	CHART POSITION
The Best of Pink Floyd 1970	1970	-
Relics	28th of June 1968	UK-32 / US-152
A Nice Pair	18th January 1974	UK-21 / US-36
Tour '75	1975	-
A Collection of Great Dance Songs	23rd of November 1981	UK-37 / US-31
Works	18th of June 1983	US-68
1967: The First Three Singles	4th of August 1997	-
Echoes: The Best of Pink Floyd	5th of November 2001	UK-2 / US-2
The Best of Pink Floyd: A Foot in the Door	7th of November 2011	UK-14 / US-50
Creation: The Early Years 1965—1972	11th of November 2016	UK-19 / US-103

SOUNDTRACKS

TITLE	RELEASE DATE
Tonite Let's All Make Love in London	8th of July 1968
Zabriskie Point	9th of February 1970

SINGLES

1967

Arnold Layne / Candy and a Currant Bun

See Emily Play / The Scarecrow

Flaming / The Gnome

Apples and Oranges

1968

It Would Be So Nice / Julia Dream

Let There Be More Light / Remember a Day

Point Me at the Sky /

Careful With That Axe, Eugene

1969

The Nile Song / Ibiza Bar

1971

One of These Days / Fearless

1972

Free Four / Stay

1973

Money / Any Colour You Like

1974

Us and Them / Time

1975

Have a Cigar / Welcome to the Machine

1979

Another Brick in the Wall (Part II)

1980

Run like Hell / Don't Leave Me Now

Comfortably Numb / Hey You

1982

When the Tigers Broke Free /

Bring the Boys Back Home

1983

Not Now John / The Hero's Return (Parts 1 and 2)

1987

Learning to Fly / Terminal Frost

On Turning the Away / Run Like Hell (live version)

One Slip / Terminal Frost / The Dogs of War

1994

Take it Back / Astronomy Domine (live version)

High Hopes / Keep Talking"

Keep Talking / One of These Days

1995

Wish You Were Here (Live)

2014

Louder Than Words

PINKFLOYD A Kaleidoscope of Conundrums